IF YOU'RE NOT THE LEAD DOG, THE VIEW NEVER CHANGES

IF YOU'RE NOT THE LEAD DOG, THE VIEW NEVER CHANGES

A Leadership Path for Teens

William R. McKenzie, Jr.

Copyright © 2011 by William R. McKenzie, Jr..

Library of Congress Control Number:		2011915602
ISBN:	Hardcover	978-1-4653-6088-5
	Softcover	978-1-4653-6087-8
	Ebook	978-1-4653-6089-2

A percentage of this book's profits will go to children's charities

This book was printed in the United States of America.

To order additional copies of this book, contact:
Xlibris Corporation
1-888-795-4274
www.Xlibris.com
Orders@Xlibris.com
102697

CONTENTS

PRAISE FOR
IF YOU'RE NOT THE LEAD DOG, THE VIEW NEVER CHANGES

'As a parent with children moving towards middle school and high school, I was thrilled and grateful to find a book written for and speaking directly to kids this age! Parents need to give their children the critical tools to become successful leaders in society, and those tools are found in Bill McKenzie's book!' – Caroline Jones, mother and business owner

'As an outdoor professional working with children and young adults for over 20 years in adventure education, I am always looking for resources that provoke a forward thinking agenda for my staff and program participants. Bill McKenzie's book gives you the tools to assist any young adult in making changes toward a more positive and successful life!' – Andrea K. Galioto-Evans, Associate Director and YMCA Camp Professional

'This is breakthrough material! Every teen and parent should read Bill McKenzie's book. It's a tremendous blueprint for a teen's successful future!' – Ben Roberts, owner Foundation Fitness

'Bill McKenzie brings leadership fundamentals to life by addressing them from the perspective of a college athlete, CEO, triathlete and father. The outcome is a leader's handbook; an insightful, practical and uniquely personal resource that engages the leadership potential in all of us!' – Ashlie G. Bucy, Chief Branding Officer, Redgrave LLP

'Leadership comes naturally to some. The rest of us need help learning how to lead, and the earlier the better. Directing his thoughts to middle school and high school students, Bill McKenzie has provided students with a good place to start. Like algebra and composition, leadership skills can be taught, and the timing couldn't be better for needed leadership.' Jack Dillard, Marketing Consultant

This book is dedicated to the memory of Eve Carson, Morehead scholar at the University of North Carolina at Chapel Hill, 2004-2008. Eve set an example for outstanding leadership that is inspirational to all, regardless of age.

And when you get the choice to sit it out or dance,
I hope you dance . . . I hope you dance.

—Lee Ann Womack, country singer

Teach this triple truth to all: a generous heart, kind speech and a life of service and compassion are the things which renew humanity.

—Buddha

An education is the key to success. Bad habits and bad company will ruin you.

—M.Sgt. Roy Benavidez, Medal of Honor winner in Vietnam, Mexican American and part Yaqui Indian

"Cheshire Puss," she began rather timidly, "would you tell me please which way I ought to go from here?" "That depends a good deal on where you want to get to," said the Cat. "I don't much care where," said Alice. "Then it doesn't matter which way you go," said the Cat.

—Lewis Carroll, *Alice in Wonderland*

In the shopping malls, in the high school halls, conform or be cast out. In the basement bars, in the backs of cars, be cool or be cast out.

—Rush, *Subdivisions*

The best way to predict your future is to create it.

—Raul Villegas, under-thirty Mexican attorney and ultrasuccessful network marketer

Every morning in Africa a gazelle wakes up.
It knows it must run faster than the fastest lion or it will be killed.
Every morning a lion wakes up.
It knows it must outrun the slowest gazelle or it will starve to death.
It doesn't matter whether you are a lion or a gazelle.
When the sun comes up, you better start running.

—African proverb

I have a very blessed life. I think anytime you're making a living at what you love to do, you're blessed. That's what I try to instill in my kids. Go after what you really love and find a way to make that work for you, and then you'll be a happy person.

—Tom Petty, front man for Tom Petty and the Heartbreakers (sold fifty million albums)

People spend their whole lives dreaming of becoming happier, living with more vitality and having an abundance of passion. Yet they do not see the importance of taking even ten minutes a month to write out their goals and to think deeply about the meaning of their lives. Goal setting will make your life magnificent. Your world will become richer, more delightful and more magical.

—Robin Sharma, *The Monk Who Sold His Ferrari*

If what you're doing today isn't getting you where you want to go, change what you're doing. It's what leaders do.

—Ben Roberts, young entrepreneur and owner of Foundation Fitness

We should learn to disagree without being disagreeable.

—President Barack Obama

ACKNOWLEDGMENTS

Books are never solo efforts, and this one is no exception.

There have been countless people, all leaders in some capacity, who have sparked my interest in the subject over the years. Some have been good leaders, some have been not so good, and a rare few have been world-class. To all these journeymen and journeywomen, you have my eternal gratitude for lessons learned.

Ashlie Bucy was the first to tackle the raw manuscript, and she did it with serious interest and energy. Her foundation's focus on leadership development for teenage girls is making a major difference in young lives, and her critique of this book was invaluable. Ashlie, you helped get the ball rolling, and I am forever grateful.

To friends Caroline Jones, Jack Dillard, and Andrea Galioto Evans, my most sincere thanks for your critique, your candor, your time, and your intelligence. Your days are busy, the demands on your time are heavy, but you did for me what all strong leaders do; you found a way to work on yet another project. You guys are the best.

Lifelong friends come in many different forms, and Pat Meisky's gut interest and launch support in this project has been significant. One of the best examples of servant leadership that I know of, Pat has leadership qualities he hasn't even touched yet. I'm confident he will.

We are truly blessed when that rare individual appears in our life, someone who leads us to places we never thought possible. Marisa Carter has led me to the edge; I just need to take the next step on yet another amazing leadership journey.

Having witnessed the recent evaporation of much in American business, watching the cataclysmic changes unfold, and wondering if much-needed leadership will ever resurface, I want to thank business associates Jim and Priscilla Harrison for reassuring me that all is not lost in the leadership world.

They are an incredible team, exemplifying the absolute best that people have to offer one another via energy, passion, focus, and compassion. All of corporate America could learn from Jim and Priscilla.

To my wife Sally, much thanks for letting me break the bank on one leadership book after another over the years. We all make sacrifices in life, big and small, but yours has been larger than planned. Thank you for your support, understanding, and putting up with some "unreasonable thinking."

And to our two children, Will and Sarah, you were important players in the genesis of this book. When I saw the awesome leadership potential in you both, I knew the struggles and the triumphs had to have serious meaning for others. You guys are my favorite leaders. Carry on.

INTRODUCTION

Let me get right to the point of this book.

This book is about leadership for middle school and high school students; nothing more, nothing less.

This book has a singular focus: to make students aware of how critical the concept of leadership is to their personal happiness and success.

I have been there, done that; it may have been a different time in history, but lots of teen challenges nonetheless. Yes, times have changed; personal, family, and societal issues may now have different priorities and obstacles, but the need to be an effective leader remains paramount. So whether it's 1967 or 2011, some things remain the same.

This book covers ten key leadership attributes. There are certainly many more, but I have chosen a select ten that I think every young adult should master to become an effective leader, not just for their school years, but for a lifetime beyond.

Leadership is, without question, one of the more critical ingredients to anyone's personal and professional success. There simply is no substitute. If we all desire to achieve some measure of happiness and success in our lives, then becoming an effective leader is a must.

It's time to step up and make a difference: become a strong leader.

This is not a lengthy book. I have purposely kept each chapter short and to the desired point. There is no need to overcomplicate this important subject. We have a habit of doing that in American society today, overanalyzing and complicating the simplest of concepts. Leadership, in and of itself, is not an overly complex subject.

The reasons behind this book are straightforward. The landscape in America today, whether in business, education, sports, politics, religion, or within the family, is facing unprecedented stress and disruption. The reasons are many and varied, but there seems to be at least one common denominator, and that is the weakening—and, in some cases, the total absence—of *effective leadership*. This is a crisis with profound consequences, many of which are at play as this book is being written.

The need for students to get a grip on what it takes to become an effective leader has never been more important.

The luxury of a twenty-year business career to figure it out is long gone. And while student involvement in such worthy endeavors as scouting, the YMCA/YWCA, church youth groups, athletic teams, and school clubs can go a long way in nurturing basic leadership skills, the day has come to demand an acceleration of exposure and acquisition of serious leadership attributes.

This brief and concise look at the importance of leadership should fit any student's ability to comprehend and put into action.

My sincere hope is that students will find something of value in this book. Something that might change a life for the better, something that might add a missing spark to family or school, team or club, individual or group.

Read carefully, read thoughtfully, read joyfully, and strive to be the lead dog in whatever you choose to do in life. The trip is worth taking.

"If we choose not to change, then we have made a choice, and that is to stay the same."

A Word to Students

This little book about *leadership* could have a big impact on you.

Maybe your mom or dad bought you this book and said, "You need to read this. It's important. We want you to succeed in middle school and high school and everything that follows."

Or maybe you bought this book yourself (awesome)—no prompting, no suggesting, no mandate—you're just interested in taking charge of your life, making it as good as it can possibly be.

Regardless, here's the deal.

A lot of stuff is important in life, but at least *two* things *really* matter:

Your happiness and your success, and that's what this book is ultimately about.

After all the late-night studying for good grades, after all the athletic-team participation, after all the hanging out with friends, after all the dates wished for and dates received, after all the first cars, after all the good friends made and maybe some lost, after all the after-school jobs, after all the success and after all the disappointments . . .

You need to be happy. You should be happy, and your success goes hand in hand.

How you got this book is somewhat inconsequential. The fact that you have it *is* consequential.

The potential consequences after reading this book are huge. They're exciting, they're about taking charge, they're about making things happen, they're about creating change, they're about becoming a catalyst, and they're about achieving lasting happiness throughout your life.

You know, there's a lot of *noise* in the world today. You'll want to move away from the constant distractions that clutter daily life. Make this a priority. You'll learn how as you read this book.

Don't confuse this noise with real challenges. You, no doubt, are aware of some of the incredible issues you face today. Here are a *very few* that will require not only your awareness but also your attention in some manner:

➢ You and your friends spend 7.5 hours a day watching TV, playing video games, on a cell phone, texting, or tweeting.
➢ Sixty-six percent of eighth graders cannot read at grade level.
➢ Ninety-two percent of eighth graders are below average in math proficiency.
➢ Fifteen-year-olds rank near the bottom out of thirty-four of the most developed countries in math and science.
➢ The dropout rate in high school is 30 percent nationwide and is as high as 75 percent in some metropolitan areas.
➢ One student drops out of high school every eleven seconds.
➢ Violence in middle and high schools continues to escalate; teens assault teachers daily and bully fellow students to the point of suicide.
➢ Many high schools are no more than "failure factories."
➢ Drug and alcohol use are epidemic in most high schools.
➢ Teen pregnancy rate in the USA leads all other developed countries.
➢ Almost 20 percent of American youth live at the poverty level.
➢ Twenty percent of teens are obese, and that number is growing rapidly (*obese* meaning at least thirty pounds over your target weight).

Recent data coming out of education at the college level is horrifying. One reputable survey found that 36 percent of students demonstrated no significant improvement in learning after four years of college. No improvement in the areas of critical thinking, complex reasoning, and written communication. This equates to educational bankruptcy.

A recommendation regarding your education—you need to view the 2011 movie documentary *Waiting for Superman*. Make this a priority, and take it very, very seriously.

Your world is now changing at mind-blowing velocity, and the throng of competition you will face for the desired high-paying jobs and flexible lifestyle is no longer clearly defined. A college degree is not the guarantee it once was. The corporate structure that your parents may know so well has now begun to crumble. You will need to master a different set of skills:

- ➤ Networking
- ➤ Adaptability
- ➤ Resiliency
- ➤ Self-motivation
- ➤ Accountability
- ➤ Personal branding
- ➤ People-building skills
- ➤ *Leadership*

Remember, you can live without Shakespeare and you can be happy without mastering calculus, but you can't make it in this world without critical-thinking skills and a lot of common sense.

Ultimately, your happiness and success will depend not on the things you have but, rather, on how you choose to live your life. The quality of your life will rest on how you live *emotionally*.

Learning to become a strong leader will be a key to your happiness and success, so embrace these challenges and enjoy a meaningful life.

It's all up to you. You have a choice. If you choose to become a good leader, then read on.

And remember, if you're not the lead dog, the view never changes! Think about it!

I don't like negative air. I don't like bad air!

—Lance Armstrong, seven-time
Tour de France winner

ATTITUDE

It's all about doing your best.

—Julia Mancuso, twenty-five-year-old member
of the 2010 Olympic US Ski Team and
two-time silver medalist,
2006 Olympic gold medalist

Egos are not attractive.

—Beyoncé Knowles, aged twenty-eight,
pop singer, Grammy winner,
and ultrasuccessful businesswoman

Attitude: posture; a mental position or feeling with regard to a fact or state

Great attitude is the key to great leadership.

This is the one thing you must have every day.

And it needs to be a *winning* attitude.

Outstanding leaders have a *winning attitude*; they are true champions of making good things happen.

You *must* develop a *winning attitude* and never compromise for anything less.

Attitude separates real leaders from everyone else.

Attitude attracts people to your ideas.

Attitude gets you through difficult times.

Attitude solves problems.

Attitude wins ball games.

Attitude makes money.

Attitude makes friends.

Attitude instills self-confidence.

Attitude nurtures teamwork.

All good leaders embrace a winning attitude, or they go nowhere fast.

Without an all-out champion attitude, you will never achieve the outstanding results you're truly capable of.

Again, it's that simple. It's that important. A winner's attitude is the key to leadership success.

The greatest human freedom is the freedom to choose one's attitude. (Viktor Frankl, Holocaust survivor)

Believe me, the world is littered with very talented, bright, and ambitious people who never quite got it, never reached their goals, and couldn't understand why. They worked hard, made great grades in school, kept their noses clean, did well in college, got a head start with a great job, but suddenly found themselves struggling in the business world and had no idea why. Or they never reached their potential in high school or college because of nothing more than a lackluster, trying-to-be-cool-all-the-time attitude. Yes, they were bright, they were good athletes, they thought they worked hard; but their mental approach to getting things done was often borderline negative, sometimes arrogant, maybe aloof, just getting by with minimal effort and with even less winning attitude. And they just didn't get it. They didn't understand why all of a sudden they're not out front, they're not achieving, they're not getting results, and they're not winning friends. They're not winning, period.

Their attitude sucks. Yes, it can be that simple.

You'll no doubt see some of your friends play a number of personality roles over the course of your school years. Some will perform the above, trying to project that really-cool-all-the-time attitude. It's not really them, but they can't seem to let go of the need to be cool. It becomes their identifying personality. Problem is, it rarely moves you forward in life. It's certainly not a leadership characteristic that amounts to anything substantial.

You will also see fellow students who have very controlling personalities, the ones who have to be the center of everyone's attention all the time and in every situation. They're real attention hogs. They have the I'm-the-boss mind-set and may be viewed as strong leaders. Wrong. It's one thing to be ambitious. It's totally another matter to have to control every situation you find yourself in. Nobody really wants to follow someone whose sole mission in life is to be the number one hot dog.

One of the key attributes of effective leadership focuses on an attitude of service, of making yourself available to help others, not to control them. This is a very powerful concept and one we'll talk more about a little later. Think about it: service versus control. Which environment would you rather work in?

It's all a matter of attitude.

Look around you. How many of your friends and fellow students consistently display a winning attitude? Do your teachers convey a winning attitude? How about your coaches? Your principal? And what about your parents? If anybody should be leading by example with a winning attitude, it should be Mom and Dad, right?

A piece of advice: if the important people in your life are not quite up to your expectations in the winning attitude department, don't be too quick to judge. Losing good attitude periodically is easy to do. It happens to all of us at some point.

But good leaders always regroup and get attitude back on track.

First, always look inward. Make sure that you're on track with great attitude. Lead by example. You'll be surprised by the power of change that a winning attitude can impart on others. This is a key element to becoming a strong leader—the power to change people and events. Attitude is the first place to start. Get it right and so will your friends and family. And if they don't, it'll be their loss, not yours. You'll be the winner, and that's always a great feeling.

Your attitude has the power to change a lot of people and life events, to create meaningful change for both yourself and others.

And that gets us right back to the concept of embracing an attitude of servant leadership—helping others overcome obstacles, helping others solve problems, helping others see things your way—the way of a winning attitude.

Winning attitudes are a lot like leaders: they aren't born (we'll discuss this in more detail later, but leaders are, in fact, not born that way); they're nurtured, cultivated, and learned over time. And anyone can accomplish getting a winning attitude. It's a mind-set, it's a state of awareness, it's a matter of wanting to go in that direction, realizing that anything less will eventually doom you to an uncomfortable state of mediocrity.

Embracing a winning attitude is kind of like deciding what sport you might like to play. If you really want to play, not just make the team, then you'll have to possess certain qualities that will separate you from others competing for playing time. You're the only one who can make that decision. Do you want to play, or do you just want to make the team? Do you want to become an effective leader, or do you want to have others always in control of what you do, how much money you earn, where you live, where you go to college, what you will major in? It's entirely up to you. You can be a player, you can develop a winning attitude, or you can settle for letting someone else dictate your life's important needs and direction.

The Japanese Way

It's very likely there is a made-in-Japan car in your driveway (actually, it might be manufactured outside Japan, but the engineering originated there). Their reputation for auto quality and engineering efficiency is almost legendary.

One of the hallmarks of Japanese business culture is the concept of attitude among its employees. In fact, that focus on attitude can be traced back to the samurai warrior class in medieval Japan. In the samurai period beginning in the twelfth century, one's skill with a sword was often a matter of life and death, and it was acknowledged that the greatest masters of the sword were those who first learned and mastered the right attitude. It was said that a master swordsman could quickly judge the skill of an opponent by his attitude, even before that opponent made his first move.

When Japanese corporations interview job applicants, the first thing they look for and measure in that applicant is their attitude. Candidates must have the right attitude, regardless of how otherwise brilliant or talented they may be. In promoting employees, Japanese companies rate attitude as the top attribute. In the Japanese business world, the right employee attitude includes such attributes as being a good listener, polite, observant, humble, cooperative, and determined. This has given the Japanese business culture a decided advantage over their American counterparts. While most Western professional athletes learn very quickly that a great attitude is key to their successful performance, many Western businesspeople have not yet learned just how powerful the right attitude can be in their personal and business lives. For those fortunate ones who have embraced the concept of a winning attitude, they have found their lives to be healthier and far more productive. And fun!

Want to be in control of most of life's situations? Become an effective leader, embrace a winning attitude; and that will create a meaningful life for you, your family, and your friends.

Attitude over Obstacles

Speaking about being in control of your life, just witness the accomplishment of Arizona State's Anthony Robles.

Anthony won the 2011 NCAA wrestling title in the 125-pound division with a final round 7-1 decision over defending champion Matt McDonough of Iowa. This capped an undefeated 36-0 season for Robles, who was also named the tournament's outstanding wrestler. And guess what?

Anthony Robles was born with only one leg.

Anthony wrestles with one leg, no prosthetic substitute.

What kind of an attitude do you think Anthony had to develop over the course of his young life, not just to become the NCAA wrestling champion, but also to be a shining example to others who faced similar obstacles in life?

Remember, there are no halfhearted champions in life. Just ask Anthony Robles.

The message is very simple. A winning attitude goes a long way in getting you where you want to go. A winning attitude will tag you with strong leadership potential. A poor or mediocre attitude is a virtual program for failure, without question. Don't believe it? Cop a bad attitude for the next thirty days and see how much fun you have. Better yet, choose to have a winning attitude in everything you do and see what changes it brings.

If every day you produce positive thinking, good ideas, with understanding and compassion; if every day you practice loving speech; if every day you do good actions, you know it yourself. Your value will reveal itself to the people around you. (Thich Nhat Hanh, Vietnamese Buddhist monk, 1967 Nobel Peace Prize nominee)

Be a winner. Be a leader. Embrace a winning attitude in all that you do.

Making a Difference: Eve Carson

By all accounts, Eve Carson was a very special individual. To say she constantly thought of others is an understatement. Her list of service to others is more than impressive; it's exemplary. Her leadership ability and commitment to excellence in all that she did is a never-ending example of servant leadership.

As the student body president at the University of North Carolina at Chapel Hill in 2008, Eve was the total student and then some. She attended UNC on a prestigious Morehead scholarship and was a member of the Phi Beta Kappa honor society while majoring in political science and biology, her sights set on medical school. As a North Carolina fellow, she was also part of a four-year leadership development program for undergraduates.

Teaching and working with children were important service interests for Eve. In 2006, she taught science at Frank Porter Graham Elementary School in Chapel Hill as part of UNC's INSPIRE program, whose mission is to encourage young students to pursue science as an interest. She also served as a tutor at Githens Middle School in Durham, North Carolina, and served as an assistant coach in the Girls on the Run of the Triangle, a character-development program for girls aged eight to twelve that uses running to teach values and a sense of self.

Eve didn't confine her leadership mission to the UNC area. In her sophomore year, she spent a semester in Cuba and went on to do volunteer work in Ecuador, Egypt, and Ghana. Back on campus, she became involved in Nourish International, an organization started by UNC students in 2002 for hunger relief.

Eve was a winner, always displaying a winning attitude. Eve led by example, a true servant leader.

On March 5, 2008, just prior to her anticipated graduation in May, Eve was robbed at gunpoint and shot to death in Chapel Hill by two men, one only seventeen years old.

Leadership attributes learned: passion, winning attitude, serving others

Attitude Key Points

➢ Be a winner through your daily attitude.

➢ Use mental muscle—be resilient and positive in the face of negativity.

➢ Stay away from negative people; they can't help you.

➢ Focus on what's positive every day, not what brings you bad air.

➢ Find something positive in your friends and make them feel special because of it.

➢ Celebrate success, no matter how small; this breeds a winning attitude.

Whatever you do, do enthusiastically and people will like you.

—Chris Martin, lead singer for Coldplay

PASSION

Believe.

—the word imprinted on seventeen-year-old
high school tennis player Melanie Oudin's tennis shoes
at the 2009 US Open Tennis Championships, where she
defeated the number 29 and number 4 seeded players

I just like to challenge myself to do things that I don't think I can.

—nineteen-year-old pro surfer Bethany Hamilton
(lost her right arm to a tiger shark attack
while surfing at age thirteen)

Passion: strong feeling; emotions as distinguished from reason; an object of
affection or enthusiasm

Let Passion Drive You

At 9:58 a.m. on Thursday, May 22, 2003, professional golfer Annika
Sorenstam teed off on hole number 10 at Colonial Country Club in Dallas,
Texas, in the PGA's Bank of America Colonial Championship. By doing so,
Annika became the first female golfer in fifty-eight years to play in a PGA
event. Annika's desire to play that day had all the elements that might
make a lesser person crumble in fear—risk, intense focus, killer attitude, and
making a change required. It would have been easy to politely decline the
invitation, quietly accept the compliment on her incredible achievement as
a lady professional golfer, and continue in her own comfort zone. But she

stepped outside that zone and accepted—no, welcomed—the challenge with absolute *passion* for the game of golf. While she missed the thirty-six-hole cut, Annika more than exemplified what it means to have passion for what you do in life. Hers was an outstanding display of incredible leadership within the sport of golf, for both men and women. It was one of the most exciting sporting moments I have ever witnessed. It was a true leadership moment.

Passion in leadership is a big deal, a really big deal.

If you don't have passion, if you don't have enthusiasm for what you're doing, why do it?

Passion is the link between who you are and how well you want to perform at some task, some subject, some sport, or some other identified goal.

Don't have passion? Then don't waste your time or mine on trying to lead me anywhere. I won't follow you, and neither will anyone else unless you are *passionate* about what you're doing and where you're going as a leader.

How Can Passion Make a Difference?

Do you think Michael Jordan was passionate about playing basketball? He won six NBA championships and is considered to be the best basketball player ever. *The best ever.*

Do you think seventeen-year-old Melanie Oudin is passionate about tennis? The high school tennis player qualified for the 2009 US Open Tennis Championships and made it to the fourth round by defeating seeds number 29 and number 4. She had the word *believe* imprinted on her tennis shoes.

Do you think Michael Phelps is passionate about swimming? He once went five years without a day off from practice and won eight gold medals at the 2008 Olympics. He is the greatest Olympian in history.

Do you think twenty-year-old Trevor Marsicano is passionate about speed skating? He fought through years of being bullied as a child, coming home from school with choke marks on his throat, to make the 2010 Olympic US Speed Skating Team.

Do you think Danica Patrick is passionate about race car driving? She was the first female driver to compete in the Brickyard (Indy) 500 in 2004. At twenty-six, she was the first female to win a Formula 1 race in 2008.

Do you think JK Rowling is passionate about writing? Her Harry Potter books made her the first billionaire author. Yes, billionaire.

Do you think Lance Armstrong is passionate about cycling? He won seven consecutive Tour de France races while battling cancer. Think about it one more time—seven consecutive years and had cancer. In 2009, at age thirty-seven and after three years of retirement, he finished third in his Tour de France comeback.

Do you think Shaun White is passionate about snowboarding the half pipe? He won Olympic gold medals in 2006 and 2010 at age nineteen and twenty-three, doing tricks never thought possible in that sport. He turned pro at age thirteen.

Do you think fifteen-year-old Taylor LeBaron is passionate about health? Weighing in at almost 300 pounds at age fourteen, Taylor decided to make a change. With passion and dedication, he lost 150 pounds, and in 2009, while still a high school student, he wrote a book about it, *Cutting Myself in Half*.

Do you think thirteen-year-old Jordan Romero is passionate about mountain climbing? In May 2010, he became the youngest climber to successfully summit Mt. Everest, the world's highest mountain at just under thirty thousand feet. With one more climb in Antarctica to go, Jordan will become the youngest to achieve the revered Seven Summits. He set this goal when he was nine years old.

Passion requires you to get excited about something. It's where excitement meets opportunity.

That's right, excited, an elevated state of feeling. All strong leaders bring passion to their business whether that business is a high school, a university, a football team, a new business start-up, a church, or a Fortune 500 company. If those in charge, those in leadership positions, really intend to achieve desired results, they know they will have to bring passion to their operating agenda. They will have to be excited about the business strategy they have chosen, and they will have to excite and lead their employees, their teammates, their faculty, and their students.

Leaders lead by example, and if they don't have *passion* for what they're doing, you'll know it, and you'll look elsewhere for strong leadership. So if you don't have passion for what you do, don't expect anyone to follow you. You wouldn't.

Look Around

How many of your classmates who are truly excelling at academics, sports, volunteer work, church involvement, or some other chosen area of personal interest are doing so in a low-energy mode with little demonstrated excitement? That's right; they're not. No one really cruises through and accomplishes anything that resembles some state of excellence, some state of accomplishment, without announced passion. It just doesn't happen. Want to be cool and just hang out? Exert little effort and even less passion for something? Go ahead. See how far that takes you. Talk about a boring ride through life. Without passion, without excitement, without energy for something that interests you, you just won't be in a position of leadership. You won't be out there making things happen. You won't be calling the shots. You won't be leading. And that's not going to be fun.

Don't confuse passion and excitement with a given type of personality. In other words, if you're reserved by nature, if you're not the outgoing type, if you're not a talker, that's fine. You can still be passionate about something that interests you. In fact, some of the most effective leaders are the ones who work behind the scene, quietly making things happen without drawing a lot of attention to themselves, often giving recognition to fellow team members and staff.

Remember that previously mentioned concept of servant leadership? It all ties in once again with *passion*, just as it did with *attitude*.

The most effective leaders are often not the most vocal ones, but they are the ones with great attitude and great passion, however they choose to display those qualities.

Having passion for a cause does not automatically make you a leader. As you will see over the following chapters, leadership requires a number of well-defined traits, and passion is but one. But you simply cannot be an effective leader without strong passion for what you do. Passion is essential.

You've got to find what you love. Stay hungry. Stay foolish.
(Steve Jobs, Apple Computer founder and iPod creator)

Making a Difference: Bethany Hamilton

Bethany was born February 8, 1990, in Kauai, Hawaii, to parents who loved to surf. Bethany easily took to the ocean water and watched her surfing abilities quickly progress. At age eight, she won first place in a junior division of a Quicksilver surfing contest. At the same age, Bethany won first place in both a short-board and a long-board division at a tourney on the island of Oahu. At the age of nine, she began to compete more seriously, placing in the top three consistently at area-surfing championships. She quickly picked up a major sponsor, Rip Curl, which helped her plans to become a professional surfer.

On October 31, 2003, Bethany went for an early morning surf with friends. Around 7:30 a.m., she was lying sideways on her surfboard with her left arm dangling in the water. Suddenly, a fifteen-foot tiger shark attacked Bethany and ripped her left arm off just below the shoulder. Doctors said that if the shark bite had been a mere two more inches in, the attack would have been fatal. Losing almost 60 percent of her blood, Bethany was helped back to shore by friends, where a tourniquet was fashioned out of a surfboard leash; and she was rushed to the local hospital. Her dad was scheduled for knee surgery that same day, but Bethany took his place in the operating room.

Just three weeks after losing her left arm, Bethany returned to surfing, teaching herself to surf with one arm.

The following year, in July 2004, Bethany won the ESPY Award for Best Comeback Athlete. She was also presented with a special courage award at the 2004 Teen Choice Awards. In the same year, Bethany published her book, *Soul Surfer*, to detail her remarkable comeback from personal tragedy.

In 2011, Soul Surfer *was released as a major motion picture.*

In 2005, Bethany took first place in the NSSA National Championships. In 2008, she began competing full-time on the Association of Surfing Professionals World Qualifying Series, finishing third in her first competition against many of the world's best women surfers.

Here are some of Bethany's key success strategies:

> ➢ Focus on what's important.
> ➢ Face your fears.
> ➢ Push yourself to do what you think you can't.
> ➢ Be joyful.

Bethany leads with passion. She did what all strong leaders do—they find a way to overcome significant obstacles to achieve the goals they have set. In the face of overwhelming odds against success, Bethany found a way to move forward with winning attitude and great passion for the sport of surfing.

Leadership attributes learned: passion, focus, overcoming obstacles, perseverance

Passion Key Points

➢ Become enthusiastic about something important to you.

➢ Set goals and pursue them with energy and excitement.

➢ Study people you admire; see how they achieve uncommon results.

➢ Believe in yourself.

➢ Challenge yourself.

➢ Find happiness in little things; share that happiness with others.

If you chase two rabbits, both will escape.

—Unknown

FOCUS

It takes discipline and focus.

—Beyonce

Focus on what's important.

—nineteen-year-old Bethany Hamilton,
author of *Soul Surfer*

Focus: to concentrate

The ability to focus on the task at hand is critical to good leadership.

A Running Focus like No Other

If you know anything about the world of sports, you know that African runners literally dominate the sport of marathon and cross-country running. It's not uncommon for Kenyan runners to take most of the top finishes in the Boston and New York City marathons in times that virtually obliterate most of the elite field. Kenyan Geoffrey Mutai won the 2011 Boston Marathon in a stunning two hours and three minutes.

Their success can certainly be traced to an incredible work ethic where they run 150-175 miles a week at 6,000-8,000 feet elevation. It's not in their mentality to run easy. But equally important to their training schedule is the degree of *focus* they bring to each session. One of their coaches said, "The runners' lives are stripped of all diversion and comforts that Western athletes consider essential." In other words, their emphasis on training to be the best runners in the world has led them to bring an intense focus on simplifying their lives while training.

They live together in spartan training camps, many without electricity or running water. They focus on running, nothing else. There are no restaurants, no movie theaters, no banks, no dry cleaners, no malls. They leave their families for months at a time, live in primitive huts, go to bed at dark, and rise at first light. They eat simple foods. They train all day, every day. They run hard with no distractions. Western elite runners have attempted to train with the Kenyans over the years and invariably cut their regimen short. Why? They simply cannot bring the same level of focus to their daily training. They can't keep up mentally. The Kenyan runners bring more focus to the sport than anyone else in the world. The results are there for all to see. Perhaps they listen to the following African proverb:

> Every morning in Africa a gazelle wakes up.
> It knows it must run faster than the fastest lion or it will be killed.
> Every morning a lion wakes up.
> It knows it must outrun the slowest gazelle or it will starve to death.
> It doesn't matter whether you are a lion or a gazelle.
> When the sun comes up, you better start running.

Simply put, they are *focused* like no other athletes in the world are, and their accomplishments are unparalleled. The Kenyans are true leaders in the world of running. They know what focus is.

While you may feel the Kenyan story is an extreme example of focus to achieve results—and it is—it by no means clouds the reality of what all good leaders need to have. Most leaders will never live in conditions like Kenyan runners do, nor will they need to make the same extraordinary sacrifices to be the best they can be, but the parallel exists. If you want to be the best leader you can be, you will have to embrace the concept of strong focus on the project at hand. You must bring a concentrated effort to the table every day. And if you think about it, it's probably not that difficult to do. Why? Because if you're *passionate* about what you're doing, then it's fun. And if it's fun, it probably isn't hard work to you, at least not on the surface. Focusing on something that you enjoy and have fun doing may not be that hard to do.

Always think focus, just as you think attitude and passion.

A Samurai Warrior

The amazing success story of Japan once again illustrates the power of intense focus relating to leadership and accomplishment. During the samurai era, one's diligent focus on matters of importance achieved virtual cult status. It amounted to "being Japanese" and became synonymous with completing any task undertaken. The Japanese believed themselves to be superior to anyone else in focus and work ethic. Those beliefs became culturally ingrained in Japanese society and would eventually emerge within Japanese business circles, giving their workforce a competitive advantage over many Western business cultures. Their ability to bring intense focus to solving problems and listening to their customers has made them the perennial leaders in the automotive industry.

What does all this have to do with you becoming a leader?

You can't accomplish any desired goal without being focused.

- ➢ Are you striving for top grades and acceptance to your choice of colleges and universities?
- ➢ Are you working to save money for college?
- ➢ Are you setting sights on making the next high school all-American basketball team?
- ➢ Are you trying to build solid friendships?
- ➢ Are you planning to audition for a school play?
- ➢ Are you trying to master playing a musical instrument?
- ➢ Are you targeting to initiate a new school tutoring program?

Guess what? *It all requires focus.* Good things just don't always happen; you plan and set goals, and you focus on what it is you want to accomplish. And the ability to focus will eventually set you apart from those who won't, and then you are on your way to getting a leadership edge on everyone else.

All good leaders have the ability to focus on goals and objectives.

It's a basic requirement for leadership success. You can't pass it off to someone else. You can't delegate focus. How good is your best teacher? How good is your best coach? You have to know they're incredibly focused on what they do. That's a key reason they're so good at what they do. They bring concentrated effort to the subject every day. They're on top of their game.

They're leaders in the truest sense. They're getting results. How? Well, you just said they are your best teachers and coaches. Their passion and attitude and focus simply deliver what you consider to be outstanding results. You see it every day.

Ask them what drives them to be the best they can be. Ask them about leadership, about attitude, about passion, about focus. Listen carefully to what they say. It's no accident they're as good as you think they are. Let them tell you why.

Isn't that what leaders do, deliver outstanding results? And they can't do it without focus.

Focus Requires Filtering

In his acclaimed 2005 book on management, leadership, and individual success, *The One Thing You Need to Know,* leadership consultant and author Marcus Buckingham writes the following:

> To thrive in this world will require of us a new skill. Not drive, not sheer intelligence, not creativity, but **focus** . . . to be able to focus well is to be able to filter well. Today you must excel at filtering the world. You must be able to cut through the clutter and zero in on the emotions or facts or events that really matter. You must learn to distinguish between what is merely important and what is imperative. You must learn to place less value on all that you can remember and more on those few things that you must never forget.

"We all struggle in the area of focus," writes former pro triathlete and author of *How Lance Does It,* Brad Kearns. "Even motivated people see opportunities coming from so many different directions that it diverts their attention. When people are not focused, they make excuses beforehand to protect themselves from the pain of failure, and that becomes a vicious cycle."

No doubt the great teams of Kenyan runners have accomplished this leadership task quite well. They have successfully filtered out what isn't necessary in their quest for success in distance running. Rather, they have identified what is imperative and have brought tremendous focus to their goal, eliminating wasteful distractions along the way.

This Is What Leaders Do

This is what you can do. Keep focus in mind. Write it down, put it on your leadership list of attributes to remember, skills to work on. You can focus, you can filter through the clutter of everyday life, you can eliminate wasteful time, and you can experience exciting success as you develop strong leadership skills.

Remember the Kenyan runners, look at your best teachers, and watch your most successful coaches. They all exhibit great focus in what they do. It's one of the reasons you admire them as much as you do. It's one of the reasons you enjoy being around them.

So learn to focus on important goals and objectives. It doesn't mean you have to live in a box. Being focused is about staying on a deliberate path, owning that path, making it your path. It'll pay big dividends for you down the road.

The mind is everything. What you think, you become. (Buddha)

Making a Difference: Marin Morrison

Marin was raised in Florida and, at an early age, took to the swimming pool quickly, like a lot of other children in the Sunshine State. By the time she was in the fifth grade, her family moved to Atlanta where she joined the Swim Atlanta team. At age thirteen, she beat seventeen-year-old Amanda Weir, who would go on to win two silver medals in the 2000 Olympics. Her coach said, "Marin has all the tools, speed, desire, coachability. We're pretty much talking unlimited potential."

Attending Collins Hill High School in Suwanee, Georgia, Marin set numerous school records and appeared to be well on her way to the US Olympic Team Trials-Swimming. However, at the state high school championships, Marin became ill and finished way off her expected times. She complained of a searing headache and vomited on the pool deck. A visit to a neurologist resulted in the discovery of a plum-sized brain tumor. The tumor was successfully removed and declared benign. But months later, the blurred vision and pain returned, and an aggressively growing tumor was discovered once again. There was no choice but to operate. The prognosis was bleak, and Marin was left paralyzed on her right side. The tumor was malignant.

Even with this horrifying news, Marin remained determined and focused. Her first words following intense speech therapy were, "Can I still swim?" In

Defer no time, delays have dangerous ends.

—Shakespeare, *Henry VI*

URGENCY

Everyone admires the bold; no one honors the timid.

—Robert Green and Joost Elffers,
48 Laws of Power

Do, or do not. There is no try.

—Yoda, *Star Wars*

Urgency: immediate action; calling for haste

Do You Act with a Sense of Urgency?

All good leaders work against planned timelines. And that's not a burden. It just makes sense.

If you're training to make your varsity football team, you don't just get around to it whenever. You work against a schedule, either one you set or your coaches set or a combination of the two. There's a sense of urgency to train in preparation for the upcoming season, or the likely consequence will be a losing one. Preparation and urgency are vital.

In their fascinating book *48 Laws of Power,* authors Green and Elffers made a relatively simple but powerful observation when they said, "Everyone admires the bold; no one admires the timid." Any leader that is bold has an attendant sense of urgency about what he/she wants to do. Otherwise, nothing gets done in timely fashion, schedules fall apart, the people you want to lead don't see you getting things done, and your effectiveness as a leader is greatly diminished.

Don't misunderstand me. I'm not suggesting you live your life on an all-out roller-coaster ride daily, trying to knock off one project after another at the speed of light. How much can I get done? How fast can I do it? No, that's not the point. Good leaders are certainly in tune to being bold and getting things done quickly, but they do so with organization and planning. They do so with *attitude, passion, focus, and urgency.* It's the concept of doing right things right as opposed to doing right things wrong. You want to do a good job of doing the right thing; and you want to get it done, most of the time, as quickly as possible. You want to work smart, not hard.

Certainly, there are times and projects that call for a longer and more protracted timeline. As I just said, leadership is not about spinning your wheels at warp speed every day. Good leaders do a great job of planning, setting strategy, and putting the right team together. They know where they're going and how they're going to get there, even through failure. But they don't kill a lot of time in the process. There's no real dead time. Things keep moving forward, the goal is in mind—attitude, passion, and focus are at work, and so is a sense of urgency. Yeah, Larry the Cable Guy calls it "get 'er done," and he's about right on.

Good leaders don't waste a lot of time. They make things happen, sooner than later.

The Little Bighorn—Urgency and Survival

Sitting Bull and Crazy Horse, the two best-known leaders of the Lakota Sioux Indian nation, wasted little time in setting battle strategy against General George Armstrong Custer and the Seventh US Cavalry in June of 1876. Having lived through one broken US government treaty after another, having seen their tribal lands invaded and ravaged repeatedly, having seen their magnificent bison herds slaughtered by the tens of thousands, having witnessed what today we call genocide, Sitting Bull and Crazy Horse had an *extreme sense of urgency* to plan what perhaps would be their last stand against the relentless invasion of white soldiers.

It wasn't enough that they were smarter in battle tactics than Custer and his officers; it wasn't enough that the Sioux were more focused on survival than on their white counterparts. The ultimate winner of the Battle of the Little Bighorn would need to bring more battle strategy into sharper focus *faster* than Custer and company. Indeed, on that hot day in June 1876, the leadership edge went to Sitting Bull and Crazy Horse in virtually every aspect of warfare known at that time.

49

Sitting Bull was extremely organized in both short- and long-term strategy. He was able to bring several disparate Indian tribes into cohesive teamwork through his reputation as a warrior (leader), as a strong communicator, and as a leader with vision. He didn't waste a lot of time. Once he established a strategy, once he crafted a plan, the execution of that plan happened quickly and completely. And if anyone doubted Crazy Horse's sense of urgency in matters, they only had to think about the origins of his name.

He made things happen quickly, maybe too quickly for some, but Crazy Horse always displayed imaginative initiative in battle, and there was no mistaking his sense of urgency when it came to the survival of his people. He was also one of the most humble of all Sioux warriors.

Sitting Bull and Crazy Horse, along with numerous other very capable Indian leaders, completely annihilated General Custer's famed Seventh Cavalry at the Bighorn River in 1876. While it was a short-lived victory for the besieged American Indian, it serves as a crystal clear example of outstanding leadership, embracing the qualities of *teamwork, focus, and urgency* to accomplish a defined goal—in this case, the ultimate goal, one of personal and family survival. Custer was simply outled by his Indian counterparts. Their sense of urgency to survive must have been far greater and in sharper focus than Custer imagined and planned for. Sitting Bull and Crazy Horse were bold leaders; there was no room for the timid in their culture, and history regards them both as exhibiting some of the very strongest of leadership qualities.

> Success most often goes to the person who sees that he has made a mistake and quickly changes. Winning leaders are invariably good 'game coaches,' because they are the first to see how things are going, then quickly figure out why, and then they make the appropriate changes. (Michael Ledeen, noted *Wall Street Journal* writer, *Machiavelli on Modern Leadership*)

Note the phrase above, "then quickly figure out why." It's the urgency factor surfacing again. Sitting Bull and Crazy Horse were superb "game coaches" at Little Bighorn. They had to be; it was a matter of survival.

Dell Computer—Change or Perish

It's highly likely you or someone in your family own a Dell computer. Once known as the direct sales innovator in home computers, Dell developed a business culture often referred to as a culture of bureaucracy, meaning that over time, Dell essentially lost their ability to change quickly to successfully address market demands. Their business model was simply too unresponsive, too slow, too nearsighted. Profits fell a staggering 51 percent in one quarter in 2006, and the trend continued into 2007. Michael Dell, the once highly regarded founder, was named one of 2006's worst leaders by *Business Week* magazine, who cited him for "worst reaction time" for his inability to move away from and transform the lethargic Dell culture into a more responsive organization. While Dell was mired in slow motion, rival Hewlett-Packard increased sales 26 percent in 2006. Dell's sales fell another 14 percent that year.

Michael Dell finally got the message and, in 2007, was quoted as saying he would change the company into one that was "bold in thinking and *swift in action.*"

- ➤ Swift in action
- ➤ Quickly figuring out why
- ➤ Good game coaches
- ➤ Making the appropriate changes

The ability to act decisively and with urgency is a leadership skill you will need to develop.

Urgency can certainly be linked to initiative. People showing initiative in any endeavor seem to display an inherent sense of taking charge to get something done. They don't wait to be asked, they don't waste time, they don't procrastinate, they don't forget—they move on it *now.*

Leaders that seize the initiative are impatient but in a good way. And in taking the initiative, a distinct sense of urgency invariably surfaces.

Again, look around at your classmates. Who's out front on select projects? Who's taking charge on the soccer field? Who's organizing the next Spanish Club meeting? Whoever is leading those efforts is showing both initiative (taking charge) and a sense of urgency (making it happen in timely fashion—speed), both hallmark attributes of strong leaders and two characteristics that seem to link together quite well to help leaders get results.

You now have four leadership tools: *attitude, passion, focus, and urgency.* Is that enough? Well, it's a great start, but you'll need a few more.

Making a Difference: Teens in Palm Beach City, Florida

In the summer of 2009, a group of restless teens in Palm Beach City, Florida, were growing tired of having no money, some not old enough to find summer jobs, others old enough but unsuccessful in finding employment. Their neighborhood had an 86 percent poverty rate, one of the highest in the state. So with seemingly limited options to have a productive and fun summer, what did these teens do? They jumped on a great project with an immediate sense of urgency!

They decided to find a way to improve their neighborhood by learning to plant a major garden, one with herbs, fruits, and vegetables. Wanting to earn money, the teens saw their efforts as a means to earn money and, at the same time, help others in the poor neighborhood. They would teach others the benefits of eating healthy and, in the process, would upgrade their neighborhood.

What did these leadership-focused teens learn?

The kids learned about economics, discovered the joy of helping others, put a run-down neighborhood to good use, experienced the excitement of making a profit, and became good leaders in the process.

Leadership attributes learned: focus, urgency, creativity, overcoming obstacles, serving others

Urgency Key Points

➢ Be bold and aggressive in a good way.

➢ Don't delay decision making.

➢ Up your energy level when completing a goal.

➢ Initiative is important; take charge and move a project forward.

➢ See if a to-do list works for you, or maybe a not-to-do list.

➢ Move through distractions; don't get sidetracked and delayed.

Teamwork. They slam that word at you every other minute. *Teamwork. Teamwork. Teamwork.*

—Marcus Luttrell, US Navy SEAL

TEAMWORK

Whatever I have to do to help my team, that's what I'll do.

—Broderick Hicks, senior cocaptain, number 24 ranked
Wake Forest University Basketball Team

America is in all kinds of trouble—from Wall Street to Main Street. Why? Perhaps because we've lost the ability to work together, even for profit. Our inability to work together . . . is undermining America.

—Warren Bennis on leadership,
Managing People Is like Herding Cats

Teamwork: the activity of a number of persons acting in close association as members of a unit

What's wrong with the American political establishment today? Three words: *lack of teamwork.*

Democrats—lack of teamwork.
Republicans—lack of teamwork.
Our government's basic problem—lack of teamwork.

Ask any astute businessperson today what key attributes an employer looks for in future employee hirings, and you will invariably hear the word *teamwork* mentioned. *Employers must hire people who can work together as a team.* It's not a nice-to-have quality in the workforce. It's an essential necessity that, if absent, will eventually spell failure for any given business today.

Why is teamwork so important to the principles of excellent leadership? Why do all *effective* leaders focus on outstanding teamwork as part of their personal operating behavior?

It's a New Day

The days of the general commanding the troops in business, industry, school, etc., are long over. Getting desired results in any business enterprise, educational or otherwise, no longer relies on a single hero and a thousand helpers. Why? Life is simply too complex and too difficult for any one person to totally run the show. It can't be done effectively or successfully by any one individual. In a fast-paced world, working in a team concept can be enormously helpful. It's a virtual necessity for any leader to develop and nurture solid teamwork. You can't do without it.

Yes, you have a head track coach, you have a high school principal, you have a senior minister—there's someone in charge. But ask these people if they expect to carry out their daily functions in solo fashion. I am sure they will be quick to tell you how important their supporting staff is, how vital their team is to the overall range of responsibilities they are charged with, how important it is that *teamwork* be used to achieve outstanding results in the jobs that they do.

Simply put, teamwork is critical to any measure of personal and collective success, and effective leaders must know how to develop it and use it constructively to achieve targeted results.

It's less me and more we.

Examples of effective teamwork are virtually everywhere you look today. Perhaps the most recognizable ones are in the world of sports, for the obvious reasons. Most athletic contests involve teams; and the drama, while often focusing on one or more key team members, eventually comes back to the *team* as a whole. Even in more solitary sports like golf, the athlete usually has a team of people—caddy, swing coach, head coach, short-game coach, and so on. He can't be successful without his team working together to do what they do best to support his goal of winning.

Does pro golfer Phil Mickelson have a team working with him? Absolutely. Phil knows the value of teamwork. He hasn't won forty-plus tournaments, four majors and achieved a number two world ranking by himself. Oh, and Phil won his first pro tournament as a nineteen-year-old amateur. *Phil knows teamwork.*

Climbing the World's Tenth Highest Mountain

If ever there was a sport that required incredible teamwork to achieve success, it's the sport of high-altitude mountain climbing, or mountaineering. Imagine what it took Arlene Blum in 1978 to lead the first ever women's attempt to climb the world's tenth highest mountain, the Himalayan giant Annapurna, at 26,545 feet. She had to begin by picking a top-rate climbing team, women that not only had all the technical skills required but also could put personal ego aside and realize that individually, they may or may not make the mountain's summit. That call would eventually rest with Arlene as the climbing leader. But there would have to be an incredible amount of teamwork to have any chance at success against such a dangerous and challenging mission. Her team was successful, but only a few of the climbing team made it successfully to the summit. The climb took the ultimate in sacrifice and teamwork, but the goal was achieved.

The Ultimate Team: US Navy SEALs

You've heard of the Navy SEALs (Sea, Air, and Land)? They are one of the most effective fighting teams in military history. Here is what one nationally known consultant says:

> The SEALS are without doubt one of the highest-performing organizations (teams) on the planet. The secret ingredient is that every SEAL is a leader/teacher, engaged in continuous, interactive teaching and learning. (Cannon and Cannon, *Leadership Lessons of the Navy SEALS*)

The SEALs operate in teams. They train together in teams for a minimum of eighteen months and then continue their teamwork as mission orders demand. *They don't conduct solo missions. They always function as a well-trained team, and that is perhaps their greatest strength.* Their military accomplishments are legendary for the degree of danger and operating difficulty they encounter and successfully overcome. They are the military team that vows to leave no team member behind, whether dead or alive. That's the ultimate commitment to teamwork.

On April 9, 2009, a three-man SEAL team rescued American boat captain Richard Phillips from Somali pirates by firing three simultaneous nighttime gunshots from a moving boat in choppy water. Three shots, three kills. This type of skill level is truly amazing, the necessary teamwork to accomplish such a feat even more so. Working together, following a carefully crafted plan, believing in each team member's ability and focus, these SEALs made the seemingly impossible a reality. Their secret? Mental conditioning and *teamwork*.

In the early morning hours of May 1, 2011, SEAL teams dropped into a walled compound in Abbottabad, Pakistan, a stealth mission to take out the world's number one terrorist, Osama bin Laden. Forty minutes later, it was mission accomplished. Bin Laden was dead, and all SEAL teams were back to home base unharmed.

Once again, we see the power of teamwork in the most difficult and dangerous of circumstances.

Want to lead like a SEAL? Take a look at the six key values SEALs focus on:

1. Put teammates first — *How do I treat others? How do I fit into the team? What is my responsibility? No matter your profession or goal, ask yourself these questions.*
2. Second-guess yourself — Quitting something happens to everyone. Ask who you are.
3. Allow yourself to fear — Fear is a shared experience; you'll get a lot of energy from those around you. It's OK to be afraid. Recognizing that is the first step to overcoming it.
4. Control your emotions physically—Ask a friend to study your posture when you're happy or content. Then practice it over and over. Your psyche will follow your body.
5. Break big goals into small targets — Try to stay in the present. How do you eat an elephant? One bite at a time.
6. Have faith in yourself — *This is the most critical part of mental toughness. Have faith that you'll figure it out.*

I like number 1 and number 6. These two SEAL values can take you a long way to becoming an outstanding leader. And teamwork is so vitally important.

Not by Yourself

Think for a minute of your own personal experiences in trying to accomplish some goal—at home, at school, at your after-school job, on an athletic team, in your church youth group. How many times did you finish the task at hand all by yourself? For sure, there are times when it's like, "Well, if I don't do it, no one else will," and you go ahead and get it done. Great! You just took charge, you just showed initiative, focus, urgency, hard work. But you can't do that time after time. Sooner or later, the job at hand will require something bigger than just you.

Teamwork will be the key to completing the job, reaching the goal, getting results.

Entire books have been written about the value of working in teams, and still, a lot of seasoned businesspeople just don't get it. How successful do you think your favorite sports team will be without outstanding teamwork? It takes more than one great point guard to win a high school championship. It takes more than one super halfback to win football games. It takes more than just one family member having a great attitude to bring happiness and joy into your entire family. It's a *team effort*, every day, every week, every month, every year.

There isn't a successful business or happy family functioning today with only one person in a leadership role. It takes *a team of people*; whether that team is only two people in a family or two thousand people in a corporation makes no difference.

Success requires leadership. Leadership requires teamwork. It's a pretty simple equation.

Making a Difference: Kenneth Ledbetter

"I just had that desire, that passion to be somebody else different than what I was," said nineteen-year-old Kenneth Ledbetter, describing his feelings at the death of his mother when he was only ten. Kenneth is a young man with purpose despite some of his past setbacks.

In addition to losing his mother at age ten, Kenneth lost an older brother in 2005. Kenneth ran with the wrong crowd, sold drugs to survive, and eventually wound up homeless. He had no idea where his next meal was coming from. And finally, it was critical decision time. He could continue the reckless and dangerous path to nowhere; or he could step up, get a healthy dose of the three Ds as he says—*determination, dedication, and discipline*—and move in a different direction.

So in June 2008, as he reflected on his recent high school graduation from High Point Central High School in High Point, North Carolina, Kenneth was excited to talk about his recent trip to California to talk about his successful involvement with MOVE, a youth leadership group at High Point Central that promotes nonviolence on school campuses. The after-school initiative also teaches goal setting, *teamwork*, self-control, etiquette, drug prevention, and political awareness.

"It changed my character all over again," said Kenneth. And in the process, Kenneth overcame serious obstacles to become a leader by example. He made a conscious decision to take charge of his life, to do the right things, to become *focused*, to get a *winning attitude*, to help others in the MOVE program. And in doing so, Kenneth Ledbetter, at age nineteen, became a *servant leader* and a *team player*.

Leadership attributes learned: passion, focus, overcoming obstacles, creating meaningful change, serving others, teamwork

Teamwork Key Points

- ➤ Learn to work with and through people; not over, under, or around them.

- ➤ Remember, it should be less me, more we.

- ➤ Be like a Navy SEAL; put teammates first.

- ➤ Many problems are simply too big for one person.

- ➤ Use your athletic experience—mediocre team or great team?

- ➤ Reflect on your favorite teacher or coach; what did they do extremely well?

I took a few steps today, and I'm grateful.

—Colleen Clyder, age fifteen,
brain cancer survivor

Balance

Do you want to be really happy? You can begin by being appreciative of who you are and what you've got. Do you want to be really miserable? You can begin by being discontented.

—Benjamin Hoff, *The Tao of Pooh*

Life moves pretty fast. If you don't stop and look around once in a while, you might miss it.

—Ferris Bueller, *Ferris Bueller's Day Off*

Balance: mental or emotional stability

Catch a Breath

We've just covered some pretty deep stuff, some very important stuff, a lot to absorb, a lot to think about. So let's take a small break and talk about how to keep all this stuff in the right perspective. Let's talk a little bit about the concept of *balance*. Happiness is certainly a part of leading a balanced life, and we'd all like to be happy, no question.

I walk a lonely road, the only one that I have ever known. Don't know where it goes but it's only me and I walk alone.

The above line from Green Day's award-winning 2006 CD could easily describe any leader's feelings on a given day. Leadership can be a very lonely walk at times. The responsibilities, whether real or self-imposed, can weigh

avily on you. People are depending on you, people are waiting to hear
om you, people are ready to follow you. Make a mistake and some people
will jump all over you. Do a great job and some people will say it really was no
big deal. Yeah, you can't please all the people all the time. And good leaders
know they can't run a perpetual popularity contest.

Leadership is not a popularity contest!

Leadership can sometimes be very lonely and very stressful, but it
comes with the territory, as they say. Do you want to do something easy or
something great?
So what can you do about it?
Look for *balance* in your life.
Repeat. Look for *balance* in your life.

So Life Is Tough

Let's face it. Even if leadership were not on your agenda, school and
family would be a full plate.

If you're headed to college, you no doubt are taking (now or later) college
prep courses, AP courses, honors courses, or similar. And these are demanding
subjects. Most teachers assign some amount of homework daily. If you have an
after-school job, you might not get home till supper at six or seven o'clock to eat
quickly and then do your homework. If you're on an athletic team, same schedule.
And if you're chairman of a school club, in a Boy Scout *troop*, doing volunteer work
at the hospital, tutoring disadvantaged children, taking piano lessons, going to
dance, etc., it's ten or eleven o'clock before lights out—on a good night.

Then you start it all over again the next day.

How do you get balance in all this? How do you become a leader and still
keep some measure of sanity? Let me offer a few proven suggestions.

Keep a Sense of Humor

Sure, life is serious, grades are important, your soccer team wants to
win them all every year, parents expect a lot, teachers are demanding, and
friends are sometimes not too friendly. You just have to

> ➤ back off the seriousness of everything for a moment,
> ➤ do the chill thing,

> laugh a lot—at yourself and with others, and
> watch a good comedy on TV or DVD/movie.

Every successful leader, really successful leader, has a great sense of humor. It lowers blood pressure, it makes you feel good, it relaxes you. Laughter is the body's natural medicine. This isn't hard. It's an awareness thing. Just think about it. And laugh some more.

Detach

That's right, remove yourself from the daily action, not physically, but mentally:

> Bury the cell phone for twenty-four hours.
> Forget Facebook for a while.
> Give up the tweet urge.
> No BlackBerry for a day or two.
> Take an absolute media break—it won't kill you.

Practice what I call looking in from the outside. Pretend for a moment you're not really engaged in any of this fast-paced stuff every day. Take a look around. Observe. Observe again. You're on the outside looking in. What do you see? Ask yourself how you might change what you see to calm things down.

Take a Time-Out

This is different from detachment. Detachment is a mental exercise. Time-out is a physical act. This is taking a well-deserved break. You could

> find some solitude;
> go to a movie;
> change your environment briefly;
> take a walk early in the morning before things really get going;
> go for a trail run;
> make the next church youth group ski trip;
> head for the local lake, rent a canoe or kayak, and spend some solitary time on the water;
> go to the library or a place where it's quiet and read a good book;
> take a walk on the beach or hike a mountain trail.

Just take some physical time-out periodically. Your body and mind will thank you.

Be joyful. I love surfing very much. It helps me appreciate everything I have been given. (Bethany Hamilton)

Keep Things in Perspective

Remember, while becoming a leader is important, while setting goals and wanting to achieve some measure of personal success is a good thing, nothing should ever be all consuming. You can only do so much. Don't compare yourself to the next guy. Find things that make you happy, things that hold your interest. There are many ways to experience success in school and beyond, and it's admirable to be aggressive, ambitious, and goal oriented. But too much of anything can sometimes prove unproductive. Even too much of the good stuff—sports, academics, church, family—must be kept in the right perspective. It's a key part of leading a balanced life. And always be thankful for what you have.

Be Aware of Your Happiness

Don't take being happy for granted. Don't rely on the accumulation of material things to make you happy, although it's normal to be happy with material items. Just take some time-out to think about your happiness, the people and things in your life that make you happy. Slow down and think about things and events in your life (big or small) and the people in your life (old or young) that bring you happiness. As you practice this happiness-awareness concept periodically, think about a passage from the well-known Vietnamese Buddhist monk, Thich Nhat Hanh, from his book *Touching Peace*:

> The Buddha told his students, "My friends, do not rely on anything outside of yourselves. Be an island unto yourself, and take refuge in the island of yourself." During difficult moments when we do not know what to do, this is a wonderful exercise to practice.

The World Keeps Spinning

I don't have to tell you how connected we all are 24-7. Text messaging, e-mails, cell phones, Twitter, blogs, Facebook and BlackBerrys all contribute to student overload on top of an already demanding school, family, and personal agenda. Your world is becoming more complex every year. You're constantly challenged to do things faster than before. It truly is the age of speed. Work quickly, work fast, get a lot done right away. Master the Internet, master PC technology, and do it faster this year than the last (or faster this *month* than the last). The business world you will someday face is seemingly a heart attack looking for a place to happen. It's frighteningly brutal in most places. Here are few USA business facts from recent years:

> * Workers today spend 20 percent more time on the job than they did thirty years ago.
> * One in three workers are chronically overworked.
> * The American middle class is rapidly shrinking; their buying power is stagnating.
> * The top 1 percent of income earners, the ultrawealthy, controls 24 percent of the nation's wealth.
> * More than one-third of workers are not planning on using all their vacation time.
> * Seventy-two percent of Americans report they are constantly under "extreme stress."
> * Today, stress is the leading cause of visits to the doctor's office.
> * The economies of China, India, Russia, and numerous other countries are growing faster than that of the United States.

But remember, there is always opportunity in adversity. Yes, the above business facts are something to be concerned about as you and other students begin to look ahead; but if you learn to work smart, if you master the leadership attributes you're reading about, you just might move over and around a number of career difficulties that stymie most people.

Challenges All Around

The challenge for you, for all your fellow students, and for all of us collectively, really, is to make a conscious effort to lead a balanced life as best as we can. We all must establish a set of *core values* that we will not compromise despite the never-ending pressures to do so. We all must continue to reassess our lives, take another look, do a gut check, ask the tough questions. Am I in balance? Am I happy? Am I providing good leadership to my friends, family, school, job, team, etc.? Am I getting enough downtime? Do I know how to relax amid the fast-paced demands I encounter daily? Am I laughing every day?

Your world—our world—isn't likely to slow down anytime soon, if at all. You will have to take charge of finding some measure of balance in your life. Don't wait for someone else. You can make it happen by keeping in mind some of the points just mentioned.

And again, are you happy? Remember the little book *The Tao of Pooh* and be appreciative of what you have. Keep a winning attitude, and find happiness and thankfulness in your daily life. It's all around you.

Balance and happiness go together. Have one, and you're likely to have the other. Have both, and you increase your chances of becoming a very good leader. And becoming a very good leader is a very good thing. It's what you're interested in, right? It's why you're reading this book. I hope so.

> The past is already gone, the future is not yet here. There's only one moment for you to live, and that is the present moment. (Buddha)

Making a Difference: Army 1st Lt. Brian Brennan

In 2008, twenty-five-year-old Lieutenant Brennan was a patrol leader in the 101st Airborne Division serving in Afghanistan. A roadside bomb killed three of Lieutenant Brennan's fellow soldiers while seriously injuring him. To say Lieutenant Brennan was seriously injured is putting it mildly.

Lieutenant Brennan suffered acute brain injury, collapsed lungs, internal bleeding, a ruptured spleen, multiple compound fractures of both arms, and the amputation of both legs. On a scale of 1 to 10 with the most serious injuries being a 1, doctors listed Lieutenant Brennan's injuries as a 1. Lieutenant Brennan remained in a coma until Gen. David Petraeus visited him one day, whispered the regiment's nickname in his ear, and watched in amazement as Lieutenant Brennan suddenly came out of his coma.

Awarded New Jersey's first Hall of Fame Unsung Hero Award in 2009, Lieutenant Brennan said, "I won't be happy until I'm able to do everything I did when I had legs. I can't go back to combat because it's not ideal for me to go back. So, my mission is to help other soldiers."

Having suffered so much, Lieutenant Brennan put his priorities toward helping others, and in so doing, he led by example. Having suffered so much, imagine what it took for Lieutenant Brennan to find balance in his new life. But he did it. He's the perfect example of servant leadership and finding balance in life, obstacles notwithstanding.

Leadership attributes learned: winning attitude, focus, overcoming obstacles, serving others, finding balance

Balance Key Points

➤ Be grateful for all that you have.

➤ Find time to reflect on what you're involved in.

➤ Look for periods of solitude; find some quiet time.

➤ Be joyful; look for happiness in yourself and others.

➤ Keep a sense of humor; laugh a lot, but not at the expense of others.

➤ Live in the present; follow the example of Lieutenant Brennan.

If you can change your way of thinking, you can change everything around you.

—Willie Jolley, jazz musician and author

UNREASONABLE THINKING

Every day, and on some days every hour, you in some way need to break set—take a different perspective, challenge the status quo, ask a different kind of question, see the world another way, and help yourself and your colleagues ask, "How would we really like it— how do we really need to have it?"

—Lynch and Kordis, *Strategy of the Dolphin: Scoring a Win in a Chaotic World*

You watch Bode and you see what you can accomplish by pushing the limits.

—Andrew Weibrecht, age twenty-four, unheralded US Olympic Ski Team member and 2010 Winter Games bronze medalist, on fellow team member gold medalist and ski racing legend Bode Miller

Don't tell me how many troops they have. Tell me who their Generals are.

—Napoleon, emperor of France, 1805-1814 (generally regarded as one of the world's greatest military tacticians)

Unreasonable: not rational; excessive; immoderate

Should I Be Unreasonable? Seriously?

I bet you're wondering about this concept!

How can a good leader get there by being *unreasonable*? You said the definition means being excessive, irrational, immoderate; so how can I become a really strong leader by being so out-of-bounds about things? Isn't that what's wrong with so many businesses and sports teams today? Excessive salaries, excessive egos, excessive poor behavior, excessive wrongdoing? What do you mean by telling me I should learn to be *unreasonable* to become a good leader? What's this "breaking set" business all about?

Making Changes

You've heard of status quo, which is Latin for "current state of affairs." It's things as they exist now, things as they may have been for quite some time. *It's a state where nothing is changing.*

Let's use the creative movie *Babe* to illustrate this attribute:

The scene: Christmas day on the farm. The pig, cow, hens, and Ferdinand the duck crowd by the kitchen window, craning their necks to see which unfortunate one of their kind has been chosen to become the main course at dinner. On the platter is Roseanna the duck, dressed with sauce l' orange.

Ferdinand the duck: Why Roseanna? She had such a beautiful nature. I can't take it anymore! It's too much for a duck. It eats away at the soul . . .

Cow: The only way to find happiness is to accept that the way things are *is* the way things are.

Duck: The way things are *stinks*!

If nothing is changing, there's a good chance that progress is not happening either. Meaningful change is critical to your school years, to your school success, to your personal growth, and to your stepping up to be a leader in life.

Didn't we say leadership is about change? Don't leaders create meaningful change? And don't most people tend to resist change?

So what do we mean by being *unreasonable*?

In 1989, Charles Handy, a visiting professor at the London Business School, published a book titled *The Age of Unreason*, in which he attempted to outline a new way of thinking that would better equip business and schools to deal with what he saw as massive change coming in the twenty-first century. Professor Handy was right on. Our world is changing at light's speed in 2011 and has been for quite a few years now. That course is likely to be the norm in your lifetime.

Without question, we all live in a time of great change and risk. You, as a student, are constantly faced with situations and decisions that require some measure of risk. Will you go to college or move straight to the labor pool? What are the risks of foregoing a college education? Money, job security? The emphasis today is on brainwork, and 80 percent of all jobs in the USA requires a large measure of mental preparation as opposed to physical labor to earn a meaningful salary. The overwhelming demand is for cerebral skills, not manual ones.

What's the risk of giving up two sports to focus on just one? Will it get you a college scholarship? What if you don't get one? Isn't there a risk there?

Becoming Unreasonable

In the business world, there's a term called *dominant logic*; it refers to people who possess deeply held assumptions about the world. The inference is that for these people to be successful, they'll have to learn to be more open to thinking differently to change their *deeply held assumptions* and to see the world as it is: a fast-changing mass of people and information.

Deeply held assumptions may get in the way of your ability to create necessary change, of your ability to break the status quo, of your ability to take risks and think *unreasonably.*

Tackling risk sometimes requires an *unreasonable* approach. It demands a *different* approach at solving the dilemma before you. You might need to find *options* to the risks you're faced with, and this might require a more *creative* thought process.

I use these terms—*unreasonable, different, creative*—to illustrate both the need and the value of thinking in nontraditional ways to manage the risks that will invariably come your way at school. The decisions you will face, the risks you will need to manage, will be huge. Some will be answered with little thought or effort at all. Others will demand that you get real creative, become unreasonable in thought and problem solving, as well as

- ➢ see the world in a different way,
- ➢ break set,
- ➢ get innovative, and
- ➢ forget dominant logic.

You've seen the E*Trade baby TV commercials; they're nothing short of genius, very creative, very innovative. Someone broke set and began to think differently to create a magical marketing tour de force for E*Trade. Same for GEICO's caveman commercials. What other examples of amazing creativity can you think of? Did these require a different way of thinking?

Business Is Changing

Lifelong, full-time jobs have virtually disappeared. Yes, General Motors and Procter & Gamble can show an employment roster with many twenty-five-plus-year service anniversaries, but that's a rarity in today's business world, and it's fading fast. Experts project you'll change jobs seven to ten times over the course of your working career, and that's a conservative guess at best.

Traditional businesses are thinning out, and there's a distinct shift toward home-based businesses, with thousands beginning each month. This type of ongoing change will require a new set of skills—*creativity, idea-based, change-focused, adaptability, information-based, innovation, a paradigm shift.*

You will have to become *unreasonable.* You will have to focus on becoming a leader. To have any real chance at success both in school and away, you must target to become the best leader you can possibly be. Leadership is fast approaching the realm of healthy survival. It's no longer a business luxury.

What if I told you that everything you know is wrong?

My point would be, your assumptions about the world may need creative change for you to move successfully forward.

A New Circus, New Tunes, New Cars, New Threads

Case in point might be the world-renowned Cirque du Soleil (Circus under the Sun). It's somewhat of a business paradox in that it's a circus but certainly not a traditional circus; there are no animal acts but a lot of people. People are the circus, not the animals. Yet the Cirque model is more profitable and a more sustainable model over time, one that continues to deliver circus-style entertainment. But without breaking with past assumptions of the circus, this highly creative and extremely popular venue would not have evolved. Someone was in the *unreasonable* zone when this idea took shape. They were thinking differently, asking out-of-the-box questions, and looking to create meaningful change. They were most definitely not thinking by the status quo.

Being unreasonable means embracing change, bucking the status quo. It's often referred to as *upside-down thinking* or thinking *outside the box*. It gets back to what leaders have to do to become effective—think differently; take creative approaches to solve problems; work these changes through people, not by themselves; more servant leadership; more we, less me.

Sometimes you just have to break the rules, as paradoxical as that may seem. It's what leaders have to do on occasion. Why?

Breaking rules is what happened at Apple Computer as they developed the industry-changing iPod. Many Apple employees wanted no part of this project, opting for the company to make more computers. After all, that's what Apple was known for, and their success was legendary. Why change?

But another segment of Apple employees began to look at market data, information that was telling them that people wanted mobile computing. In what has since been called market bravery, Apple took the leap and managed the risk to apply their computer expertise to a new business model.

The iPod was born, and once again, a great example of being *unreasonable* to create a new opportunity surfaced. It's what leaders do.

Breaking rules is what happened at Ford Motor Company in 2008. Rather than accept government bailout monies to combat the economic disaster facing many large American corporations, Ford charted its own path to success by listening to its customers and learning from past mistakes. Ford began to think differently. How could they make new hybrid cars, how could they radically improve gas mileage, how could they run their manufacturing plants more cost-effectively, how could they keep thousands of employees on the payroll and save their families the trauma of lost jobs?

Ford hired a *nonindustry* executive to lead the company. Ford hired an executive from Boeing corporation, a maker of airplanes. In 2011, Ford achieved record profits. Who was thinking differently? Who was unreasonable?

Thinking differently is what led young entrepreneur Pharrell Williams to team up with Tyson Toussant at Bionic Yarns to create an eco-friendly apparel company. Creating premium yarns from recycled plastic beverage bottles, Bionic Yarns is making a wide variety of consumer products ranging from backpacks to handbags to denim wear to outdoor furnishings, all environmentally friendly and equally sustainable.

Did these guys rely on traditional business thinking to create a new market? I don't think so.

Work to change the status quo; work to make meaningful change. This is what good leaders do.

Leaders facilitate the change process by sometimes breaking down what has always been in place. This may require you to be *unreasonable* for a while, asking lots of questions, analyzing the situation, pushing those in control to see things your way. You'll need to explain why your way is the better way. Be creative, think a little (or a lot) differently, detach for a while and get another perspective on the issue, think and rethink, come up with options and alternative solutions. Solicit opinions from others.

By being somewhat *unreasonable*, being *creative*, being *innovative*, you begin to drive the bus, you begin to take charge and create the change you feel is necessary.

An Awesome Catalyst for Change

Do you think Olympian Shaun White would have won gold medals in the half-pipe doing the same old tricks?

What did it take for Shaun to push the limits of aerial snowboarding maneuvers to create new energy and excitement around the sport? You better believe he did some upside-down thinking, literally and figuratively, to come up with the extreme moves he made in the 2010 Winter Games. He broke the status quo, did his *unreasonable* thing, pulled off a fully refined Double McTwist 1260, the most difficult and dangerous half-pipe move ever attempted, and now is the leading voice for that exciting sport. In fact, Shaun had enough points on his first run to capture gold in Vancouver. So why did he attempt such a risky trick with nothing at stake? "I came all the way to Vancouver to do something amazing," he said. Case closed.

As Jim Collins, the author of the intensely researched leadership book *Good to Great*, writes, "You can either follow a paint-by-numbers-kit approach to life and do what everybody thinks you should do and stay within the accepted lines, or you can decide you want to create a masterpiece and start with a blank canvas."

Want to be like Shaun? Go for it, on or off the half-pipe. The principles are the same. See if you can create meaningful change in something of serious

---

interest to you, something that has been the status quo for some time and could benefit from *your* leadership. Make it happen *your way*. Create your own masterpiece.

Congratulations on being unreasonable!

> I reject the yardstick others use to measure me. I have a yardstick of my own, one I've discovered myself, even if I find myself in opposition to public opinion. (Thich Nhat Hanh, *Fragrant Palm Leaves*)

Making a Difference: Marisa Carter

Everybody should have a friend like Marisa Carter. That is, if you don't mind being pushed to do things you never thought possible. You see, Marisa doesn't like to be told she can't do something. She can be a little *unreasonable*, but also one dynamite leader.

Marisa says she was semiathletic in high school. She tried running, she tried swimming, she tried dancing, she tried a bunch of sports, never really landing on any one sport she truly loved. Stubborn, strong-willed, and diagnosed with ADHD, she was sometimes called flakey and suffered from low self-esteem. A car wreck at age sixteen left her feeling worthless. She took up running cross-country and became interested in the human body and athletic training. As an exercise science major at Penn State, she continued to run. The more she ran, the more she liked it. Then a foot injury sidelined her for two years, an eternity for any serious athlete. In fact, most would have given up, gone on to something else.

When Marisa was able to run again, two years later, she came back with a high-octane, push-the-envelope style. She completed the Wisconsin Ironman Triathlon in 2003 and again in 2008. That's a 2.4-mile swim, followed by a 112-mile bike, followed by a 26.2-mile marathon.

And she doesn't think of herself as athletic, but she learns from her athletic pursuits. Completing a 102-mile bike race in fifty-degree pouring rain for eight hours, climbing over six thousand feet in the mountains, Marisa learned the value of not giving up, learning to push through pain and agony, and being grateful for every breath taken on a given day, no matter how tough, no matter how difficult the challenge.

Ask Marisa what her goal in life is (like all strong leaders, she knows where she's going, what she's about), and she'll tell you it's to "make a difference in people's lives through health and wellness." Marisa, at age thirty-two, is a USA Triathlon certified coach, has a BS degree in kinesiology, a master's degree in sports medicine, and a second BS degree in nursing. She is a gifted coach and teacher, someone who displays an incredible winning attitude in every task she undertakes. No challenge is too big. She's *unreasonable* enough to find a way to succeed and push her athletes to do the same.

As a coach, athlete, businesswoman, mentor, and servant leader, Marisa leads by example with infectious passion. Her winning attitude is the underlying key to her continued success in both business and athletic competition. Everybody should have a friend like Marisa Carter; everybody should see what an *unreasonable* leader can accomplish.

Leadership attributes learned: winning attitude, passion, focus, serving others, thinking upside down

Unreasonable Thinking Key Points

- ➤ Begin to think differently.

- ➤ Look for ways to create meaningful change.

- ➤ Look for ways to effectively break the status quo.

- ➤ Always ask, "Is there a better way?"

- ➤ Learn to disagree respectfully, intelligently, and with conviction.

- ➤ Think about the impact Olympian Shaun White has had on snowboarding/skateboarding.

I just want to do something meaningful.

—Usher, five-time Grammy winner,
founder of the New Look Foundation,
an organization focused on assisting
economically disadvantaged youth

COMPASSION

I was taught from a very young age that giving to others
is what we're supposed to do.

—Nnamdi Asomugha,
Oakland Raiders cornerback,
native of Nigeria

Championing a cause is in XANGO's very DNA. We began supporting
worthy charities before turning our first profit in 2002,
and that's never stopped.

—Gordon Morton, XANGO LLC founder

Compassion: deep sympathy

The Amazing Jordan Thomas

Fifteen-year-old Jordan Thomas was enjoying a great family vacation
while scuba diving off the coast of South Florida in the summer of 2005.
Here's the story in his own words:

> On August 16, 2005 while scuba diving in the Florida Keys,
> a boat propeller struck both my legs. I was sent to the Ryder
> Trauma Center in Miami where I underwent three surgeries, and I
> lost both of my legs from the calf down. I spent about two weeks
> in the hospital and returned home to undergo rehabilitation.

My rehabilitation has been tough, but I have been given every opportunity possible.

In 2007, I graduated from the McCallie School in Chattanooga, Tennessee. I was a member of the golf and bowling teams, and one of my goals in rehabilitation was to rejoin my teammates for my senior year. I am happy to report that we had a successful golf season, and it's great to be back playing golf. I have just started my sophomore year at the College of Charleston, and I am excited to be a "Cougar." Without your love and support, I would certainly not be doing as well as I am.

When I was in the hospital, I was really touched by the kids who would never be able to achieve their dreams because they did not have the money to continue their recovery and rehabilitation. Larry was one boy who had been severely burned and was recovering in the Trauma Rehabilitation Unit. He had almost no resources with which to continue his rehabilitation after discharge. To make matters worse, Larry was placed on a waiting list to go to a foster home as his parents had abandoned him. I felt great sadness about his many losses and grateful for all the loving support I have received during my recovery.

With that in mind, I have set up the **Jordan Thomas Foundation** to raise money for children with traumatic injuries who are not as fortunate as I. With my foundation, I hope to raise at least $500,000 to help these kids. I would like for you to help us reach that goal!

Once again, in Jordan's own words, here are some of the kids his foundation has touched:

Our first beneficiary of the Jordan Thomas Foundation is named Alaina and she is now 8 years old. Alaina lives near Chattanooga and when she was 2 years old, she was in a farming accident. She lost both her legs, one above the knee and the other below the knee leading to a difficult rehabilitation. She spent several weeks at TC Thompson's Children's Hospital and her medical expenses were very high. Her family was unable to afford replacement prosthesis for those she had outgrown.

From generosity of folks like you, Alaina received a new set of "legs"! I was thrilled to watch her walk for the first time on the new prosthesis and we took photographs of the event to share.

I am excited to tell you about our second beneficiary. Noah is 6 years old and an amazingly happy child despite everything he has been through. Noah was born with a serious heart defect requiring four separate surgical procedures. While recovering from his first open heart surgery at three weeks of age, Noah suffered a complication resulting in loss of blood flow to his right leg. The leg could not be saved and he underwent an amputation at the knee.

Noah has just completed his fourth and final heart surgery and has made a remarkable recovery over the past several weeks. He has been fitted with a new "leg" and a new "knee" made possible by the Jordan Thomas Foundation and generous sponsors.

Noah is filled with the joy of life despite the incredible hardships he and his family have endured. Recently, Noah asked if he could have a foot with a split toe to allow him to wear sandals like Mom and Dad. We were delighted to help and have made his life a little easier.

Leaders have and show genuine compassion for those around them.

They know that serving others makes a major impact on everyone involved and beyond, close friends and strangers alike, and that compassion is the mark of a true servant leader. Jordan Thomas is a shining example *of leading with compassion.*

The Incredible Corporation

Exemplary corporations often take lead roles in displaying compassion and showing others what servant leadership is all about. The XANGO corporation is one fantastic and amazing example.

Based in Lehi, Utah, XANGO is one of the world's leading wellness companies. This privately held company is not yet nine years old yet has earned more than $2 billion and is one of the fastest-growing companies in US history.

From XANGO's earliest days, its founders knew they wanted to do more than just earn a living—they wanted to make a difference in lives around the world. They found a way when they decided to commit a significant portion of corporate profits to worthwhile charitable endeavors around the globe.

One of the largest recipients of this corporate compassion has been Operation Smile, a worldwide children's medical charity whose network of global volunteers are dedicated to helping improve the health and lives of children and young adults through its presence in more than fifty countries. Operation Smile treats children born with cleft palates and other facial deformities. A rather simple surgical procedure, this care is often unavailable in developing countries, and those afflicted often suffer ridicule and even physical abuse. Through Operation Smile, companies like XANGO can bring life-changing results to children all over the world.

But it's more than just a financial donation made from afar; the XANGO founders truly practice *servant leadership* because they find time in their busy schedules to attend Operation Smile missions every year, visiting with the children and their families.

All US corporations, large and small, can learn from this great example of giving time, money, and energy. As you continue your leadership journey in years to come, you will find this mind-set valuable as well.

A Nigerian Story of Excellence

When you embrace and show compassion, you truly make a difference, and that's what *servant leadership* is all about. Take a look at the story of Nnamdi Asomugha, a professional football cornerback and native of Nigeria.

Nnamdi's parents fled the impoverished African country of Nigeria when he was boy. His family quickly taught him the value of giving to those less fortunate while surrounded by the beauty of Southern California, their newly adopted home. A standout student athlete in high school, Nnamdi attended the University of California at Berkley. He graduated in 2003 with a degree in corporate finance, was a standout safety on the football team, and was selected by the Oakland Raiders in the NFL draft.

Nnamdi quickly achieved success with the Raiders, making the 2006 Pro Bowl team, and was so highly regarded that the Raiders made him the highest-paid defensive back in NFL history. His reputation as a charitable giver was gaining just as much press. Among his many compassionate efforts toward others are the following:

> - Regular visits to the East Oakland Youth Development Center to tutor inner-city youth
> - Providing shoes and running attire to underprivileged children
> - Creating the Asomugha College Tours for Students, which provide inner-city achieving students with free college tours to broaden their educational experience

"My experience with the center reminded me to always have my eyes open for opportunities to give back." Nnamdi's success strategies are the following:

> - Always seek opportunities to make a difference for others.
> - Nurture a spirit of giving in your children.
> - Share your abundance, whether it's your time, wisdom, or money.

For all his charitable efforts in the Oakland area, Nnamdi has not forgotten his native home. He serves as the chairman for his family's charity, the Orphans and Widows in Need Foundation. The charity provides food, shelter, medicine, and scholarships to orphans and widows in Nigeria.

Indeed, Nnamdi Asomugha is a great example of leading with compassion. He could be spending his free time and considerable resources doing things more self-centeredly, but he chooses to lead by example.

Many church youth groups provide teens with the opportunity to go on mission trips, often to very impoverished countries. This is an excellent opportunity to truly grasp the meaning of compassion, to witness up close and personal what kind of positive impact you can have on those less fortunate than you. But you don't have to travel outside the USA to witness such misfortune. Local volunteer efforts within your community are plentiful. Do not forget this experience, carry it with you, and make it a part of your social fabric and core value system.

You are living in a world of finite resources. Compassion should not be one of those scarce resources. You have the capacity to give and serve others for a lifetime. Do so wisely and become a true servant leader.

Think about what Jordan Thomas was able to do while still in high school. Think about what Nnamdi Asomugha was able to do through hard work, focus, and compassion for others. Look at what the XANGO corporation does for Operation Smile. Anything is possible.

> The most noble thing you can do is to give to others. Start focusing on your higher purpose. (Robin Sharma, *The Monk Who Sold His Ferrari*)

Making a Difference: Taylor LeBaron

How many of your fellow classmates have written and published a book by age seventeen? How many of your friends, those that are seriously overweight, maybe even suffering morbid obesity, have lost half their weight through focus, discipline, a sense of urgency, and a winning attitude? Cutting their weight in half? Really?

That's exactly what Taylor LeBaron accomplished when, as an obese fourteen-year-old, he began a personal quest to shed 150 pounds from his 300-pound frame. It wouldn't be easy. His junk food cravings and no-exercise lifestyle led to taunts from other kids, like "Whoa, dude, you need a bra."

Running was out of the question. He got winded just walking. Taylor was a big kid early on. By the third grade, he weighed 130 pounds when most kids were less than 100. The summer before the seventh grade, Taylor topped his grandmother's scales at 297 pounds. He knew he was in trouble.

Taylor had to wear size 44 jeans, hard to find. Triple-extra-large T-shirts, hard to find. School desks were too small. Theme park rides had weight limits, and he easily exceeded them. Class projects like clearing a nature trail were not only embarrassing but also physically impossible. On a class field trip to Stone Mountain, Georgia, Taylor's classmates decided to hike one of the trails. It just about killed him. He realized the extra weight was like a virus attacking a computer. Corrective measures would have to be taken.

Just after Taylor's fourteenth birthday, his grandparents gave his family a YMCA membership, a pivotal event in Taylor's quest to begin a new life. At the Y, he would begin to understand the value of goal setting, becoming results oriented, staying focused, making sacrifices, developing a sense of urgency toward his overall health, and becoming passionate about his new goals.

Taylor began a leadership quest to become a better person by developing his whole self.

As Taylor points out in his book, *Cutting Myself in Half: 150 Pounds Lost One Byte at a Time*, nine million US teens are overweight, and the problem is escalating at alarming rates. A no-exercise and junk-food lifestyle is literally killing the youth of America. Says Dr. Mike Dansinger, noted nutrition expert,

> Today's teens are tomorrow's leaders. The future depends on you. The world, as well as your body, is what you make of it. You can lead or follow the pack. You can win or you can lose.

Fourteen-year-old Taylor LeBaron decided to seize a leadership moment and, in so doing, changed his life forever. Read his book, and it just might change yours. Taylor is a true leader; he totally gets the *L*-factor.

Leadership attributes learned: focus, urgency, passion, creativity, winning attitude, serving others

Compassion Key Points

➢ Focus on serving others.

➢ Be grateful for what you have.

➢ Become a community volunteer.

➢ Think about what Jordan Thomas has been able to do.

➢ Find a fellow classmate that could use your help.

➢ Pray for peace every day.

I know it's a challenge to try and ride 112 miles without the use of quads or hamstrings and then get off the bike and run a marathon, but I knew to change the perception of what someone with a disability can accomplish, finishing the Ironman under all the time cut-offs was a huge step not only for me, but for all the kids and adults who are out there dealing with limb loss and other challenges.

—Rudy Garcia Tolson, age seventeen,
both legs amputated at age five,
Ironman triathlon finisher and
swimming world-record holder

PERSEVERANCE

I prepared for my treatment like it was a bike race. I made cancer like an opponent that I hated and wanted to beat very badly. I believe the athletic approach, the athletic mentality, was very beneficial.

—Lance Armstrong,
from *How Lance Does It* by Brad Kearns

We had nothing but our bare hands, a few ugly clothes, some children's clothes, that was all.

—Cham Adrong, Montagnard (Vietnamese) immigrant, reflecting on her arrival in the USA in 1986 and opening a family business twenty-four years later (Cham and her husband worked for years in low-paying jobs, often working sixteen-hour days, speaking little English. In 2010, they paid for their new business in cash; no bank loans were necessary.)

Persevere: to continue a course of action in spite of difficulty, opposition, etc.

The Armstrong Factor

If I could cite one book that would give you a great example of not just what it's like to persevere as a leader but also what a comprehensive leadership picture would look like, I would strongly recommend you read the book *How Lance Does It* by Brad Kearns.

This short and exceptionally well-written book about seven-time Tour de France winner Lance Armstrong offers an inside look at what makes Lance

Armstrong perhaps the most successful, feared, and controversial athlete of this century.

In advance of hoping that you will make it a priority to read *How Lance Does It*, I am going to devote this chapter to quoting highlights from the book and, in doing so, strive to give you the full meaning of what an exceptional leader is all about.

As you read the excerpts below, remember that Lance was diagnosed with testicular cancer that later spread to his brain. This was no casual brush with death. Lance was staring at it head-on at age twenty-seven, in the prime of his bike-racing life.

How Lance Did It

"The most life-changing insight I have taken from Lance is his intense and **unwavering positive attitude.** The Lance Armstrong Foundation's 'Live Strong' motto is about spreading hope and inspiration to the cancer community and adopting a positive attitude to face difficult circumstances—to live strong in the face of adversity."

"Lance's seven Tour de France victories were a testament to his mechanical preparation and to his refusal to let outside influences demoralize or distract him. With such a **focused approach,** he was able to perform successfully even while surrounded by a pandemonium that dwarfed anything other athlete's have faced."

"What Lance has that you and I usually don't is **focus.**"

"There were certain realities in our life that couldn't be changed. We could sit around and cry about it, or we could find a way around the roadblocks. Our answer to every setback, sorrow, and upheaval has always been to **push back, try harder, be smarter.** We weren't afraid of failing—only of stopping, of giving up. Losing is worthwhile if you learn something from it, but quitting is the defeat of hope." (Linda Armstrong Kelly, Lance's mother)

"Most people don't believe the **world should be changed.** Lance is different. He understands that hills can be climbed, and he isn't depressed when, upon reaching the summit of one, he sees a larger one ahead. He's used to that. That's what Lance Armstrong stands for." (Bono, Irish lead singer for U2 and political activist)

"The biggest thing that made Lance a champion was his level of desire, which was extraordinarily high and unwavering. He was **more focused,** trained harder, and wanted to win more than anyone in the sport." (Mark Gorski, Olympic gold medalist in track cycling)

"When he lived in Spain, he'd be out training on the bike for eight hours, then come home and go out to dinner with the family, then get on the computer or phone at night and do business for an hour. Whereas you or I would look at the clock and say, 'Enough, it's bedtime.' For sure, his energy level is super high and his **attitude is always positive**, which help tremendously."

"If I'm going to get beat by a better rider, I'm going to get beat. But I will not get beat by not doing everything possible in my power to gain an advantage."

"A champion like Lance is able to assimilate past experience, both success and failure, in a **positive and empowering manner**. In contrast, most of the general population live a life filled with repeated mistakes and have difficulty with behavior modification. You **mus**t learn from experience and adjust future behavior to survive as an athlete."

"Failure and hardship can teach invaluable lessons, if you're open and willing to assimilate them. Furthermore, I think great leaders and great human beings need to operate from an automatic, ingrained, inbred reflex to **do the right thing**, to be true to a personal moral code."

"Having a **positive attitude** is also a tremendous help. To let your past empower you instead of scar you, it is necessary to **draw positive conclusions**, even from failure and disappointment, and let go of any and all negativity."

"Lance doesn't have a to-do list. **Things just get done, right now**."

"We must not forget to include Lance's defeats as part of what built his solid foundation of success."

"Lance hates losing, but he's not afraid of it."

"The world is full of people who are trying to purchase self-confidence, or manufacture it, or who simply posture it. But you can't fake confidence, you have to earn it. If you ask me, the only way to do that is work. **You have to do the work**."

"When I'm on the starting line knowing that **I've worked harder than anyone else**—that is a great source of strength and inspiration for me."

"When you live a high-definition life, you become better, stronger, and **happier**."

"Teenagers I speak to feel a tremendous cultural pressure to pursue the fast track to success, which they have been brainwashed to believe is getting good grades to gain entry into a top college, which leads to a high-paying job, which leads to the American dream of making and spending money. With that to look forward to, no wonder high school is such a difficult time for these kids."

"So how do you become bulletproofed to cultural competitive pressures with an unshakable, unconditional confidence in your abilities? *Positive attitude, clarity of purpose, and specialized intelligence are critical.*"

"It's never too late to make a career change, and it's never too early to expand your thinking beyond the normal channels of the rat race."

"Discard self-limiting beliefs and negative memories to rewire your brain for success."

"A *positive attitude* and stimulating surroundings can increase your energy."

Improve Your Performance

See if these five tips from Lance can't improve your day-to-day performance at school:

➤ "In a life-or-death situation like my illness, *I had no choice but to be positive*."
➤ "I do lose sleep over criticism at times because I care. But you have to prioritize these things—*think less about the bad stuff*."
➤ "I never heard Lance complain about anything. He would never dwell on his defeats; he would always be thinking ahead to the next race."
➤ "When it's raining, I just put on a rain jacket and go."
➤ "*Quit bitching*."

Lance has shown tremendous perseverance over the years, finishing third in the 2009 Tour de France at age thirty-seven after a three-year layoff from cycling competition. He raced again in 2010, once again bringing his arsenal of leadership skills—focus, a winning attitude, passion, a sense of urgency, balance, team work, perseverance, and unreasonable thinking—to craft another winning strategy with his new RadioShack cycling team.

Want to be like Lance?

Then make today the best day possible, and do your absolute best tomorrow and every day thereafter.

This is what true leaders do.

They stay out front and make good things happen for themselves and everyone around them.

They persevere through bad stuff, bad people, and the negativity that comes their way.

They find ways to win, just like Lance.
You can lead, just like Lance.
And what happens if you're not the lead dog? *The view never changes!*

> When you really want something, you find a way. When you don't, you find an excuse. (Taylor Flynn, twenty-four-year-old yoga clothing fashion designer)

Making a Difference: Rudy Garcia Tolson

Rudy's life was a challenge from day one. Born in 1988 with rare multiple birth defects that included crippling pterygium syndrome, a clubfoot, webbed fingers, and a cleft lip and palate, who would have thought that this child would one day set world swimming records and finish a full Ironman triathlon?

By age five, Rudy had endured fifteen operations, was confined to a wheelchair, and had little hope of playing with friends, let alone participating in sports of any kind. That's when Rudy asked his parents to approve a double leg amputation. He was just too tired of the wheelchair. He wanted another chance at life even it meant having no legs. So at age five, Rudy had both legs amputated above the knee.

"For me, having my legs amputated at age 5 was the best thing that ever happened. After the amputation a whole world of activities opened for me and today I'm a surfer, a skateboarder, runner, cyclist, swimmer, triathlete and Ironman finisher. Sport is a great equalizer."

Indeed, it is. Rudy competed in the 2004 Athens Paralympic Games where, at age sixteen, he set a new world record in the two-hundred-meter individual medley swim event in his class. In 2008, at the Beijing Paralympics, he once again set a new world record in the two-hundred-meter individual medley. And in 2009, at age twenty-one, Rudy completed the Arizona Ironman in sixteen hours and six minutes.

Rudy has helped raise over $6 million for the Challenged Athlete Foundation and has received numerous awards for his inspiration and leadership, including the Arete Courage in Sports Award and the Casey Martin Award from Nike.

To say that Rudy has shown perseverance in the face of so many life challenges doesn't do justice. Rudy has truly been a *servant leader, taking risks, pushing limits, staying focused, competing with passion and an inexhaustible winning attitude.*

"To lead by example and show others that the sky is the limit motivates me to continue to push boundaries."

If ever there was a lead dog, Rudy Tolson is the true big dog. He's the man, he's the dude, he's the killer athlete, and he's the even better human being.

Want to pattern your leadership life after someone else? You can't do any better than Rudy Garcia Tolson. (Check out his Facebook and website; google *Rudy Garcia Tolson*.)

Need we say more about what leadership is all about?

Perseverance Key Points

- ➤ Remember the importance of a winning attitude—it gets you through tough times.

- ➤ Reflect on Lance Armstrong's battle with cancer. How did he do it?

- ➤ Don't forget the power of staying focused; move through distractions.

- ➤ Look for someone in your family who has met an extreme challenge with success. How did they do it?

- ➤ Find a classmate who is struggling with a major problem. See if you can be of assistance.

- ➤ Don't forget the life story of Rudy Garcia Tolson.

Empty your mind of clutter, maintain an inner peace. Ten thousand things move around you. In detachment, perceive the cycles.

—Lao-tzu, the *Tao Te Ching*

DETACHMENT

The best managers seek to understand their people.
This is the practice of detachment.

—Lao Tzu, the *Tao Te Ching*

How could a person possibly lead a corporation
if he cannot even lead himself?

—Robin Sharma, *The Monk Who Sold His Ferrari*

Detachment: a disconnect; a disengagement; impartiality

Remove Yourself

This may, at first glance, seem to be a very strange leadership attribute.

Do good leaders really disconnect?

Do good leaders look for solitude?

Do they truly disengage from the leadership process?

They absolutely do and do so periodically for very good reason.

As you no doubt know by now, the previous nine leadership attributes we have been discussing can be a full plate of stuff. Good stuff, very good stuff, but a fair amount to digest. If you're not careful, you'll get really caught up in the leadership process, and you may lose sight of what's important as you go forward with this new information.

So what should you do when you might begin to feel overwhelmed, when you might feel a little lost with the information, when you might feel somewhat unsure about exactly how you want to use these leadership attributes to your advantage?

Detach.

Disconnect.

Not for an indefinite period of time, but for some short period. Why?

Step Outside and Look Inside

You'll find it helpful to take a looking-in-from-the-outside approach to problems and issues (see chapter 6 on balance). Think of yourself as standing outside your home and looking in the window, observing what's happening at that particular moment. You're not actively involved; you're just looking, watching, observing, maybe even doing the chill thing for a moment.

You're detached from the household action at that moment. You see what's going on; you're just not involved.

What's the benefit from looking in from the outside?

You have a chance to see what's happening without your participation. You see the particular dynamics of the group at play without you. This gives you a chance to take a breath and perhaps see things with a little more clarity. You do the chill thing and think about what you might do differently than before, how you might approach a problem or a person or a group differently to get them where you want to go, to create the change you desire. This approach takes you out of the action for a moment, lets you see things more objectively, gives you a moment to clear your head, which in turn often enables you to make better decisions.

Don't hesitate to take a time-out; get a better view of the situation at hand by removing yourself from the action. Maybe you'll see things a little differently, with more clarity and direction.

Break in the Action

In your leadership roles, there will be numerous times you will need to call a *time-out*, sometimes just for you, sometimes for your team. This is the detached or disconnect factor, that time when you step outside the process to get a better view of what's really taking place. It's a critical and vital way to know where you are in the leadership task at hand.

What's working, what's not, why? How can you make it better? What changes, if any, need to be made? What changes, if any, do you need to make in your leadership style at that particular moment?

Becoming detached periodically is integral to achieving balance.

As we discussed in chapter 6, the concept of having a balanced life is so important to becoming a strong and effective leader. We talked about taking a time-out (physical relief) and the detached element (mental relief), both vitally important to achieving and maintaining a balanced lifestyle.

It's easy to go back to Lance Armstrong as an example of how the ability to *detach* plays into being a strong and effective leader.

A quick read of *How Lance Does It* readily shows you that Lance has a serious focus on time management. To juggle all the training, the family time, the business commitments, his LIVE**STRONG** foundation, Lance has to keep potential daily chaos at a distance. To do so effectively requires him to periodically detach or disconnect, take a time-out, reassess issues and priorities, reset strategies, find better ways, and grab a mental break. By all accounts, this ability to continually realign his time commitments and strategy toward defined goals has been and continues to be the key to Lance's unparalleled success, in all aspects of his life.

Lance knows how to detach; he knows the value of looking in from the outside.

So can you.

Just do it.

> The best leader does not use force.
> The best warrior does not act in anger.
> The best officer does not fight petty battles.
> The best managers seek to understand their people.
> This is the practice of detachment

Which brings the power to lead others
And is the highest lesson under heaven. (Lao-tzu, *Tao Te Ching*)

Making a Difference: Jestin Jennings

On the weekend of May 31, 2009, twenty-year-old Jestin Jennings had to wonder just how he had arrived at the NCAA East Regional Track and Field Championships at North Carolina Agricultural and Technical State University. Arrived indeed, as the Southern Conference champion in the men's four-hundred-meter hurdles, as a dean's list student, as his fraternity's president. Only a few short years before, Jennings was headed anywhere but the NCAA. This weekend provided a moment of reflection, a disconnect from a disadvantaged childhood, but a moment in which he could continue to learn and grow within.

One of ten children, Jestin's mom was a drug addict, and he never really knew his dad. At age twelve, it hit him, "God, I don't have what everybody else has. You get up thinking, 'Nobody believes in me. Why should I? Growing up I really had no hope."

"I started to act out. I started smoking, skipping school—a lot of things that weren't right."

But Jestin was a survivor. A high school math teacher took an interest in him, and with his talent on the high school track, he landed at Western Carolina University in the North Carolina mountains, not exactly a thriving hot spot of student diversity; the school's African American population was well below 10 percent, but it was a great opportunity for a student trying to make something significant with his young life. But it wasn't easy.

As Jestin describes it, simply, "family stuff going on" led him to momentarily quit the WCU track team. "I got down, I stopped going to practice, I told Coach I was going to quit." But friends and key family members wouldn't let him. A sister and a brother reminded him of how much they looked up to him; a fraternity brother offered spiritual encouragement.

"When people say sports can make a difference, it does. It really does keep your mind off other things. When I get mad, when I get down, I always run, and I always run hard. I take it out on the track."

The track is Jestin's means of disconnecting. It allows him some time away from "family stuff," gives him that distance from the action in order to refocus, realign priorities, get a better fix on where he's going. It's what leaders do. They don't quit. They refocus.

First semester in his senior year at WCU, Jestin had a 3.67 GPA. He was president of his fraternity. He was beginning to lead by example. As he reflected back on his young life's experiences, Jestin commented, "I really care about children. I really like giving back. I really can help out. Kids don't have a choice who their parents are. To be an advocate for that child, be a voice for that child, that really makes me smile."

"For somebody who really didn't have any family support to somebody now who's going to graduate with all these accomplishments, I would want somebody to look at me and say, 'I know I can make it. If he can do it, why can't I?'"

Jestin Jennings is a winner. Jestin Jennings is a leader.

Leadership attributes learned: focus, perseverance, detachment, winning attitude

Detachment Key Points

➢ Remove yourself every now and then.

➢ Practice looking inside from the outside.

➢ Reflect on what it means to have balance in your life.

➢ Take a few minutes of time-out every day. Think about what's going on today, tomorrow, and next week. How can you influence?

➢ Avoid becoming so busy that you lose sight of what's really important.

➢ During your periods of detachment, focus on how you can better interact with others to make good things happen.

To give anything less than your best is to sacrifice the gift.

—Steve Prefontaine, legendary 1970s
University of Oregon middle distance runner

MOVING FORWARD

Be the change you want to see in the world.

—Mohandas Gandhi, leader of the civil disobedience
movement to free India from British rule in the
early twentieth century, also known as the father of India

We weren't born to follow. When life is a bitter pill to swallow,
you gotta stand up for what you believe.

—Bon Jovi, 2009 Platinum CD *The Circle*

Without question, you guys are looking at some serious stuff as you move out of middle and high school toward whatever career you may have in sight. And a lot of you won't have a clue where you want to go in life at this stage, and that's OK.

There's something to be said for trial and error, and not everyone is ready for a college education. For those who are, be ready to get seriously focused. For those who are not, take some time to think about options, likes and dislikes, academic strengths and weaknesses, particular aptitudes you may have, where you'd like to live, etc. Have a sorting-out time, think and reflect, take some time off from the school grind after graduation. But don't wait too long to make a decision. Remember, sense of urgency.

You might remember the old saying, **"Know what you want to do before someone knows it for you."**

It should be obvious by now that whatever direction you choose to go in, becoming a good leader is an absolute must. There simply is no substitute. If you want to be happy in life, if you want to achieve some measure of success, however you choose to define success, becoming a leader will have to be part of the equation.

You've heard the time-worn cliché "This ain't rocket science" more than once, and it's very true. Leadership is not rocket science. Is becoming a strong leader the easiest thing you'll ever do in life? I doubt it. Will it be the most rewarding? I'll guarantee it.

So it's a matter of choice. Leadership can be learned. Leaders are not born. Yes, there are certain personality traits that may naturally favor specific leadership attributes, but every leadership factor we have discussed in this book can be learned. Each one of you can learn to become an exceptional leader; it's a matter of choice and commitment.

I don't need to repeat the world's incredible challenges for you. You're media connected; hopefully, you're getting the score. If not, keep reading, keep listening, and keep researching. Set yourself up to be as informed about the world around you as you possibly can be. Ignorance is a sure path to failure and unhappiness.

Let me suggest that you look back at this book again and pick out two or three leadership factors that seem to fit your personality or your particular interest. Begin to think about how best to incorporate these attributes into your daily routine. Begin to see how they can work for you and how that, in turn, positively impacts your family and friends.

You don't have to jump on all ten attributes at once. Take a gradual approach. One of the biggest successes you will experience is to just be aware of these ten factors. Keeping an awareness will eventually lead to action. Practice writing your favorite leadership attributes daily. Jot them down on anything—scrap paper, your BlackBerry, your Word document, a bookmark, etc.—it takes almost no time, but it sets you up to make leadership a priority.

Keep this little book in an accessible place. Take it out for a quick review every now and then. You'll likely see that you begin to get more meaning out of specific chapters on a second or third read. Yeah, the light will come on on occasion and you'll learn something new and exciting, and that's what leadership is about, in large measure—creating meaningful change and bringing excitement and energy to yourself and others.

What you are going to find the most exciting within this leadership journey is your ability to help others.

The bottom line is, when all is said and done, people like helping others; we just don't do enough of it. We let stuff get in the way, we lose our focus, we get stressed, we don't work to have balance in our lives, we get into the blame game, we sink into an it's-all-about-me lifestyle that can become pathological and self-destructive. In short, we get sucked into the seemingly never-ending human rat race. That's no fun, and it doesn't have to be that way. You can make that change.

Keep focused on doing the right thing, not just doing things right. The key to your happiness and success are linked to understanding and implementing the chapters in this book.

> A leader is best when people barely know he exists; not so good when people obey and acclaim him; worst when they despise him. (Lao-tzu, the *Tao Te Ching*)

Want to be the lead dog? Want to have a change of scenery throughout life? You're starting in the right place with this little book.

Analyzing others is knowledge.

Knowing yourself is wisdom.

Managing others requires skill.

Mastering yourself takes inner strength.

Knowing when enough is enough

Is wealth of spirit.

Be present, observe the process,

Stay centered, and prevail.

—Lao-tzu, the *Tao Te Ching*

A Word about Narcissism

Yeah, I know, this is a hard word to spell and tricky to pronounce, but it's a real word with real meaning, and it's worth a quick mention in today's society, particularly when we talk about what it takes to be an effective leader.

The word comes to us from Greek mythology. Narcissus was a mythological hero who was exceptionally attractive, so much so that he came to disdain all others in the belief that he was the most attractive person on earth. Upon seeing his reflection in a pool of water and not realizing that it was his own, he became so absorbed with the reflection's beauty that he could not break away from the pool's edge. There he died.

Today we use the word to define a condition that represents an *inflated view of self-worth*, sometimes described as self-love and/or having an excessive interest in one's comfort or appearance. It basically describes someone who cares little about the genuine feelings of others and is singularly focused on his or herself. It goes beyond arrogance and conceit.

The problem we see in today's society is that an increasing number of people, sometimes beginning in your age group and continuing with people well into their thirties and forties, are acting out as if they are *the* only being of any importance. It's the all-about-me syndrome.

The cultural evolution of the increase in narcissistic behavior within our society is beyond the scope of this book. Having said that, let me offer you a very brief insight into this potentially very damaging behavior.

Without question, there has been an increasing trend over the past thirty years for parents to foster a high level of self-esteem in their children. The drive is on to nurture feelings of self-confidence, feelings of "I'm special," feelings of "I'm a winner," and increased feelings of self-worth. The danger has been that many parents now carry this war cry for success to an extreme. Witness plugging baby up to educational CDs at age one, having in-home tutors at age three, pulling strings to get junior into the city's most prestigious private school, and more. Many parents are known for doing Suzi's homework throughout her school years and, yes, even into college. Parents have been known to enlist SAT prep private consultants costing up to $40,000.

This has led to our country's very blurred distinction between self-worth and narcissism. There appears to be an increasing acceptance of doing whatever it takes to get ahead. It's a competitive world, right?

We all know how competitive our world has become; and you, the middle school and high school student, already know that, maybe not to the extreme older students and adults do, but you get a little bit of that picture on most days. Grades, athletics, jobs, family—it can be all-consuming, as we have already discussed.

What you should know about leadership and narcissism is that you don't need to have the latter to effectively have the former. *Studies have shown that the most successful and effective leaders are humble, avoid the limelight, work behind the scenes, work through people (teamwork), readily give credit to others, continually look for better ways to get things done, and generally are always engaged in self-improvement. Successful leaders tend to work quietly and are not self-serving media hogs. Yes, there are exceptions, but they are not the rule. Good leaders, for the most part, are not narcissistic in their behavior.*

I want to make it clear that the ten leadership principles covered in this book in no way cross over into the realm of narcissism. Having a *winning attitude* is not about arrogance and conceit, is not about self-love, and is not narcissistic behavior. Embracing a *positive outlook* is not narcissistic behavior. Feeling *self-confident*, showing *passion* for your interests, and setting lofty *goals* is not narcissistic behavior.

What *is* narcissistic behavior is feeling that you are better than everyone else, that you are, for some reason, entitled to a certain lifestyle, that the world revolves around you, and that you have no feeling for the values of anyone else. Narcissists love to be know-it-alls. Clinical studies have shown that they are so smart they even know things that don't actually exist.

Your family may be financially blessed, your parents may work exceptionally hard to earn their six-figure income yearly, you may be fortunate enough to drive a beamer; but a host of material things does not give you privilege over anyone else in society. You can have tons of self-esteem and never realize any measure of success. And just because it's a cruel, competitive world out there does not mean you have to behave like a self-absorbed, all-about-me hotshot.

This incessant feeling of entitlement is a serious disorder in our society. However, embracing the ten leadership attributes discussed in this book in no way puts you into the realm of narcissistic behavior. Remember what we said about achieving *balance* in life? Do this and there's no need for the word *narcissism* in your active vocabulary.

Narcissus died looking at his reflection. You have better things to do.

A Leadership Lesson from Susan Cagle

It was 2007, and young Susan Cagle, a twenty-one-year-old African American, had just hit the big time. She made an appearance on the Oprah Winfrey show. Nothing could have been farther from her scope of reality only a few years prior.

Susan was raised in a cult, a very restrictive, controlling, and stifling environment for a child. "We had to do everything they told us to do," she says. "We were only allowed to read the Bible and materials written by the organization."

After spending years feeling like a prisoner and yearning for some measure of freedom, Susan escaped and began a life of her own. She was a mere teenager.

"It was like, 'Oh my gosh, I've got these feelings inside me I've always felt, a hunger for knowledge, for the world, and I was told it was wrong,'" she says. "Once I started reading, it was like, 'Wow, I need to get out of this.'"

Susan made her way to New York City and took her love of music to the streets. You see, she had a *passion* for music and wanted to be a singer-songwriter. She spent the next several years developing her talent in the subway system of NYC, giving impromptu performances to whoever might listen. She surprised and delighted subway commuters with her soulful voice and guitar playing.

"Basically, the subway allowed me to connect with people. In the subways I wasn't alone."

"I realized, looking around at all the people rushing by me, that everybody has their own story. It made me realize that, wow, I don't have to use my background as an excuse to not do anything with my life."

For years, Susan played for anyone who would listen, and then fate stepped in. Music producer Jay Levine caught Susan's act in the subway, recognized her talent, was impressed with her passion for music, and soon they began writing songs together.

One of Susan's signature songs was titled "Dear Oprah," and when Oprah heard it for the first time, she just had to meet Susan in person. The song had begun as a letter Susan wrote to Oprah at age seventeen but was never sent.

"Your story inspired me, your background, how you were brought up. You're a self-made person," she told Oprah. "It was really just me pouring out my heart in my diary to you."

So what's Susan Cagle's new take on life?

"I just feel happy to be able to walk down the street and know that I'm free."

Leadership attributes learned: perseverance, focus, passion, unreasonable, winning attitude

A LEADERSHIP LESSON FROM TARYN DAVIS

Life was good at the moment.

Twenty-two-year-old college student and newlywed bride Taryn Davis had a world of joy to look forward to. She had married her best friend and soul mate, Michael, an army corporal, and his deployment to Iraq would surely go by fast. Taryn and Michael were, after all, just beginning their life together; and like all young married couples, the possibilities for a life of happiness seemed endless.

On May 21, 2007, Taryn met a uniformed soldier at the door and immediately heard the words, "We regret to inform you . . ." She knew in that horrifyingly I'm-going-numb moment that her life would never be the same again. Her one and only true love, Michael, had been killed by roadside bombs in Iraq, only ninety minutes after they had last talked.

Grief stricken, seemingly alone in her new world without Michael, Taryn received the six black boxes with Michael's belongings. As she opened each box one by one, not knowing exactly what was in each, she sifted through clothes, photos, letters, pictures, Michael's laptop, sheets, a pillow, and uniforms. She hoped to pick up Michael's scent, to capture one last grasp of the man she loved and would never see again. Taryn began to realize that she was yet another victim of the tragedy of war.

Or was she?

Over the next four months, Taryn began a mission to meet other war widows, to try to understand their grief as she tried to understand her own. In many ways, her new life was that of a military widow, but Taryn was determined to move away from the sorrow and loneliness, away from the darkness of losing the love of her life. She soon found inspiration in the lives of other women in the same situation, all looking for answers, all seeking help and support to cope with an unimaginable tragedy.

Taryn soon realized that her love for Michael was eternal, that the lessons and things her husband had said still ran through her veins; and mostly, she realized that she was not alone. Four months after Michael died, Taryn started a nonprofit foundation for war widows, creating a website that offered a forum for online support, advice, and inspiration. In no time, Taryn had reached almost a thousand women of all ages, all having lost a husband, a son, a grandson, or a friend.

Taryn did what all leaders do; she picked herself up, she looked at adversity in the eye, and she decided she would be the winner, not the loser. She embraced the concept of *servant leadership*, quietly but effectively reaching out to others, asking how she might help them, searching for ways to make a positive impact on others.

Taryn's foundation, the American Widow Project (*www. americanwidowproject.org*), is active today and serves as an amazing example of what choosing a path of leadership can do to positively impact thousands of people. Taryn created meaningful change and, in doing so, was able to touch many, many lives.

Taryn Davis epitomizes a winning attitude, compassion, perseverance, focus, passion, balance, and being a little unreasonable in the face of so much tragedy and adversity.

You can learn much from Taryn Davis. Visit her website, send her an e-mail, copy her winning attitude in all that you do.

Leadership attributes learned – winning attitude, perseverance, focus, passion, compassion, unreasonable thinking

Some Things to Think About

- Leaders are doers, activists, catalysts, action figures.
- Leaders do what others will not do.
- Leaders do what is sometimes uncomfortable.
- Leaders do for others. They help others reach goals.
- Leaders do what is sometimes unpopular.
- Leaders are always dreaming.
- Leaders are always learning.
- Leaders are always reading.
- Leaders don't pay a lot of attention to critics.
- Leaders look to make small improvements consistently. They're not after the quick home run; they know the home run happens later.
- Leaders look to be really good at what they do, *really* good.
- Leaders show great patience and focus.
- Leaders always look for opportunity in crisis.
- Leaders spend time with misfits. They know the value of thinking differently.
- Leaders look for solitude frequently. They are good at reflecting on past actions.
- Leaders do not avoid areas of life that may frighten others.
- Leaders know they will grow as they move closer to areas of discomfort.
- Leaders have *fun*!

TEN MUST-READS

1. *Tao Te Ching: A New English Version*, by Stephen Mitchell
2. *How Lance Does It* by Brad Kearns
3. *Cutting Myself in Half* by Taylor LeBaron
4. *The Tao of Pooh* by Benjamin Hoff
5. *The Monk Who Sold His Ferrari* by Robin Sharma
6. *Leadership Lessons from the Navy SEALS* by Lt. Cmdr Jon Cannon and Jeff Cannon
7. *Soul Surfer* by Bethany Hamilton
8. *Good to Great* by James Collins
9. *Fragrant Palm Leaves* by Thich Nhat Hanh
10. *The Tao of Leadership* by John Heider

Additional Recommendations

1. *Hagakure: The Book of the Samurai* by Yamamoto Tsunetomo
2. *The Art of Possibility* by Rosamund and Benjamin Zander
3. *The Lakota Way* by Joseph Marshall III
4. *The Starfish and the Spider* by Ori Brafman and Tod Beckstrom
5. *John Kotter on What Leaders Really Do* by John Kotter
6. *Sun Tzu and the Art of Business* by Mark McNeilly
7. *The Leadership Moment* by Michael Useem
8. *Warrior Politics* by Robert Kaplan
9. *Machiavelli on Modern Leadership* by Michael Ledeen
10. *The Post-American World* by Fareed Zakaria

CPSIA information can be obtained at www.ICGtesting.com
Printed in the USA
BVOW071522301012

304200BV00001B/3/P